BETHANY KEY

MANIPULATION AND MIND CONTROL

The ultimate guide to learning how to recognize dark
psychology techniques and use the secrets of emotional
intelligence and influence to your advantage

TABLE OF CONTENTS

Introduction

E very aspect of human life has two sides-positive and negative, but it depends on the human how he or she utilizes it for their good as well as for others. Consider manipulation as a part of dark psychology, and it is used greatly for the wrongdoings and harmful deeds. On the other hand, it can be utilized positively as well, but it's all in your hand how you want to utilize it. As far as persuasion is concerned, people use it in every field and part of life. For example, a salesman will always try to persuade you to buy his or her recommended product even if you do not want to. Persuasion also has two aspects of being applied. If you try to persuade a person to do something illegal or unethical, that is part of dark psychology but if you persuade someone to get out or leave a certain thing that is not beneficial in any means, let's say suicide, then you are using it for the purpose of good. Everything you do or perceive is totally in the human mind, and you are the controller of it. If you don't want to, then no one can make you do things without your will and consent. Also, it is an essential part of living life to observe your surroundings and the people who are around you. If you do not notice the small things and interpret them wisely, then you are more likely to fall prey for something negative and hazardous. Facial expressions, body language, gestures, and the words and tone used, can predict a lot about people if observed closely. If you fail to recognize such signals that are inclined towards negativity, then you will be unable to keep yourself safe from them. Dark psychology is considered to start from the point where you have no intent or motive to do things except for your self-satisfaction and pleasure, and in return, it is damaging to the other person or even the community. Every living individual has this dark side, but not all of them let that side overcome them. Once you are exposed to that side, there is no coming back. So always watch yourself and your surroundings so that you can keep yourself off of any harm. Persuasion, manipulation, and other forms of influence are ubiquitous. You can pick up on some obvious signs here and there, but there are also hidden secret ways that others control you which you might never be able to fully comprehend.

To those who aren't fully aware of manipulation and what it is all about, it is hard to see that this process takes up three steps. Most of us will just think of manipulation as one thing—there needs to be two things in addition to the act of manipulation, which will make sure that the manipulation is successful. Perhaps you are trying to sell something, maybe yourself or your brand, and you need to figure out how to get people to be more persuaded by you to help you achieve the things that you want in this life. No matter where you are or what you are trying to do, you have all the tools that you will ever need to be persuasive or influential with you already.

Before getting into this book, there are a few things that you need to know to be introduced to this topicto get into the right mindset as you read through this text. First, understand that there are no two manipulators that are alike. There are no two easily persuaded people that are the same either. Though it might seem like this sometimes, especially since you can influence a group all at once, you can't let yourself fall into a thinking pattern where you place everyone in the same category.

Don't blame yourself for not being aware of the ways that you have been manipulated in the past. Regret isn't going to do you any good in this journey, so it's best to leave those feelings of, "I wish I would have known this sooner," behind. All that you can do now is move forward, and we will help you every step of the way!

Chapter 1:

Mind Control

MIND CONTROL

Mind control is a term that is used for several psychological phenomena such as mind control, coercive control, brainwashing, coercive persuasion, malignant use of group dynamics, and a lot more. It is a psychological theory with many names. The many names given to the theory are a clear indication of the fact that there is a lack of agreement that makes

8

room for distortion and confusion, especially in the hands of those that intend to make use of it covertly for their selfish interests.

One can, however, agree with the fact that mind control easily falls under the umbrella of influence and persuasion which deals with the way people change other people's beliefs and behaviors. While some would like to argue that all falls under manipulation, it is important to take note of the missing distinctions in this argument.

It is much better to think of influence as a continuum because at one end there are the ethical and respectful influences that make room for giving respect to an individual concerning his or her rights while at the other end there are destructive influences that rip off a person's independence, identity and his ability to come up with critical and logical thoughts.

When it comes to the darker side of the continuum, we talk about cults and sects. These are the groups of people who make use of deception and mind control skills in taking advantage of its member's strengths and weaknesses to satisfy the selfish desires of the cult leaders.

There are one-on-one cults which are intimate relationships where a person manipulates and exploits others using their influence. These are cultic relationships which are a smaller version of the larger groups that may prove to be destructive as a result of the fact that all the time and attention available are directed towards a person. These relationships may come in the form of husband/wife, pastor/worshipper, teacher/student, or therapist/client.

The best way to pin a definition to mind control is to look at it from the angle of a system of certain influences that can disrupt a person at their core and at their identity level which has to do with their preferences, beliefs, behaviors, relationships, decisions and so on.

Mind control creates a new pseudo-identity or pseudo-personality for the person and can be used in several ways to the benefit of others or that of the person himself. For example, mind control can be used for the benefit of addicts while it can also be used in bad or unethical ways.

This practice is not uncommon as it is not a mystery or dark art that is known to only a select few. It is merely a combination of words and group pressures that are packaged in a way that makes room for the manipulator to create a sense of dependence on his followers. This helps the followers make personal decisions while thinking that they are independent beings who are free to decide on their own.

When a person becomes a victim of mind control, he is unaware of the influence process as well as the changes that are taking place within him.

In discussing this topic, however, it is of utmost importance to take note of certain distinctions, as some points need to be made clear.

First, mind control is a subtle but very insidious process which means that the individual is largely unaware of the grave effects of the influence that is being imposed on them. This is the reason why they typically make little change over time with the belief that they are making decisions for themselves, when all the decisions that they are making are made for them.

It is insidious because the purpose of mind control in some cases is to entrap and cause harm to the victim.

Another distinct point to note is that it is a process that doesn't just happen in an instant. It usually takes a lot of time, which depends on factors like the skills of the manipulator, the methods that the manipulator has decided to make use of, the length of time that the victim was exposed to the techniques, and other personal factors.

However, these days manipulators do not require a whole year or several months as they have become sufficiently skilled in such a way that they can control a person's mind within a few hours.

Also, there is usually force involved in controlling the minds of others. This may not come in the form of physical force but there is certainly some form of psychological and social force/pressure.

The main aim to control the thoughts of the person you are interacting with is to achieve your desired intention. You will get many things if you can take control of the other person's mind. The approach and the techniques to use will determine whether you will be successful in achieving your goal.

You need to get hold of their unconscious to influence them. Train to be a master in controlling and at times manipulating your partner's mind and thoughts. It is attainable to take control of the intention of someone. You need to apply some techniques, and you will succeed.

POSITIVE FORMS OF MIND CONTROL

When used the right way, mind control techniques can make a substantial change in your life for the better. Mind control can teach you how to do this:

REMAIN IN CHECK

If you'd let your mind wander freely, who knows where it might lead you. One of the most distracting and dangerous thoughts is that everyone tends to be leading us down a dark and negative path. Without mind control to compel you to take over and drive your thoughts in the direction you want them to go, the concentration you need to remain on top of your game may be difficult to sustain.

PROTECT YOURSELF

With proper mental control training, you can teach yourself how to become more resilient and protect yourself from the manipulator's willful ways. Mind control will improve and reaffirm your self-confidence by reminding you that you are a strong, positive, and capable person, and no one will ever make you doubt your abilities.

COMMON TECHNIQUES OF MIND CONTROL

There are different ways which people use to control the minds of others, below are some of these techniques:

SUBLIMINAL MESSAGING:

These are either visual or auditory messages that are sent to a receiver's brains to bypass the person's normal conscious perceptions. To do this effectively, the mind controller flashes these messages to the other person's brain without giving the person's eyes the chance to capture/see the image or by making sounds inaudible for the receiver's ears.

The messages are sent directly to the brain. The mind controller aims to influence the other person and they do that effectively with the use of this technique.

BRAINWAVE SYNCHRONIZATION:

For everything a person does or thinks, there is a league of neurons that communicate with each other in the brain. These neurons generate and transmit electrical signals between themselves, creating patterns that are in the form of waves, which are known as brainwaves. For different states of mind of a person, there are different resultant frequencies of these brainwaves.

Thus, the question becomes whether it is possible to get to a predetermined state of the mind.

NEUROLINGUISTIC PROGRAMMING (NLP):

This is a technique that has its basis in the idea that successful behavioral patterns can be made possible in either the self or other people through the modification of underlying thought patterns as well as interpersonal relationships or interactions.

COGNITIVE BEHAVIORAL THERAPY:

This is a therapeutic technique that may not be related to mind control, but it works perfectly when it comes to the underlying principle of the modification of a person's behavior, known as behavioral modification, based on corresponding thought modification.

HYPNOSIS:

This is a mind-control tool that is used by professional hypnotists to fish out a person's suggestible subconscious mind by moving past the conscious and analytical mind to create positive thoughts or replace old negative beliefs that the mind has held onto for a long time.

People in sports have used hypnosis successfully. It has also been used in other fields like education, therapy, as well as self-improvement to boost a person's self-confidence and get rid of phobias, fears, and bad habits. It is used for relaxation and stress relief too.

According to the National Institute of Health, hypnosis is an effective tool in the reduction of some kinds of pains which include the pain from cancer. Also, hypnosis has been proven to have some self-help benefits. It has been said to be a useful tool in any attempt to change the thought process of another person for things like persuasion, negotiation, or sales.

When hypnosis is used in this manner, it is known as conversational hypnosis which is based on the techniques created/developed by the American psychiatrist and medical hypnotherapist Milton H. Erickson.

SOME OF THE TRICKS TO USE FOR YOU TO CONTROL YOUR INTERLOCUTORS

PAY ATTENTION

Pay attention to your interlocutor, and they will have the confidence to express what they feel. That will make them pour out their heart to you, and you will have a base to get control of their mind in any direction that you want. When you get them to trust you, they will not keep anything from you. You will have the entire picture, and you will know how to approach them.

MAKE SURE YOU TALK ABOUT WHAT MAKES THEM HAPPY AND WHAT SEEMS TO INTEREST THEM

If you get into a topic and you may not be conversant about the issue, ask questions as a way to show that you are interested. Showing that the talk is interesting to you will earn you more trust. You should tolerate them even if the conversation is boring. That way, you will be in a position to control their minds. Being attentive is a way of showing friendliness, and that will mean pleasant conversation.

HYPNOTISM

It is a great approach to take control of someone's mind when used in the right way. When used correctly, it will help you put your interlocutor in a trance within the first few minutes of your conversation. It is a way of seducing them, and you will get them to act on your suggestions.

CONTROL THE GUARD

To make any progress in mind-controlling, you need to suppress the brain shield. It is the conscious mind that you need to deal within the first place. Use softer as well as subtle techniques to make sure that your interlocutor has relaxed.

Try and get them to be in your debt, and this will prove influential. It is okay if youperform favors for your interlocutor to make it simpler to control them. Doing them good from time to time will make them feel an obligation to do good in return. Doing all this will give you a better position in the way you relate. It is advantageous to do this regularly, and it will raise the perception of superiority. The superiority will allow you to access more things that are in the interlocutor's mind. You will have more power since the feeling of guilt in the other person's mind will turn them to your will quickly.

BE GOOD TO THEM

Be kind and offer multiple choices to them. There being overwhelming choices, their imagination will persuade them to try nearly all of them. Try and show them that following your idea would be the best thing for them to do. That will make them do what you want, and that will be an assurance that you already have control over their mind. Let what they imagine take over to leading them to see how your suggestion is powerful. Use imagination to find the best that you can acquire from a person.

REPEAT SOMETHING OVER AND OVER AGAIN

Repeating something many times makes it sturdy, and that means that what we perceive is what we believe to be real. If something happens several times, your interlocutor's mind will register that as being the real thing. Repetition is known to be a vital tool in helping people control the brain as well as the thoughts of others. To solidify a concept in someone's mind, you need to repeat it as many times as possible. Use the repetition approach to your advantage, and you will have access to someone's brain without them having a clue of it.

PRACTICE BEING POSITIVE

Make your ideas look as high as possible and demonstrate how they will end up achieving success. The positive technique makes you look supportive, even when you may not be. Engage in positive interaction, and no should not be an answer. A negative reply can act as a powerful distraction, and it will not give you the ability to control the other person's thoughts. Give yes for an answer even if you know that the results will be negative. That will make the people around you think that you are supportive as well as thoughtful. Spinning things toward the possible will lead you in achieving your desired results without the other person knowing that you are controlling their mind.

MAINTAIN A HARMONIOUS RELATIONSHIP

Going directly to the exact thing that you want them to do will trigger their curiosity and make them think critically. If they get active in thinking, your entire plan to control their mind may go into ruin. You will have lost your control over them which is not your primary aim. Use the best suitable methods to strengthen the link and make sure that your interlocutor trusts you. When they believe you, they will have no difficulty in putting their confidence in you.

SEEK TO KNOW WHAT MOTIVATES THEM

Pay full attention to what they have to say, and it will be appropriate if you watch their nonverbal response. You not only need to focus on what motivates them but look into the most powerful motivator. Their most crucial motivator will give a clue on how you need to put your point across. Manipulating this motivator will be the easiest as well as the best strategy to help you in controlling their minds. What they give the most value when it comes to decision making will be of great importance. Try and remember the steps that they have used before to make decisions and try to manipulate them.

CREATE CONFIDENCE

You must let your interlocutor view themselves as being the hero. It serves as an excellent way to convince them to do what you want without them noticing you have taken control. Demonstrate to your interlocutor their perception matters in your context. When you achieve having their confidence, you will address anything to them with a lot of ease. Tell them how important it would be for them to be directly involved in your ideas. You need to tell them that they will own the credit once the ideas become successful.

MAKE USE OF THEIR EMOTIONS

There is an approach that you can apply to how somebody feels so that you can control them. When someone has mixed feelings, they may not know that they are monitoring them. They will do what you want to be propelled by what they feel.

You can use a situation that you know has addicted your interlocutor to make them do what you desire. Anger can also be an excellent weapon to take control of someone. Use a wise way that will not alarm them of your aim to induce irritation in your interlocutor.

Chapter 2:

Types of Mind Control

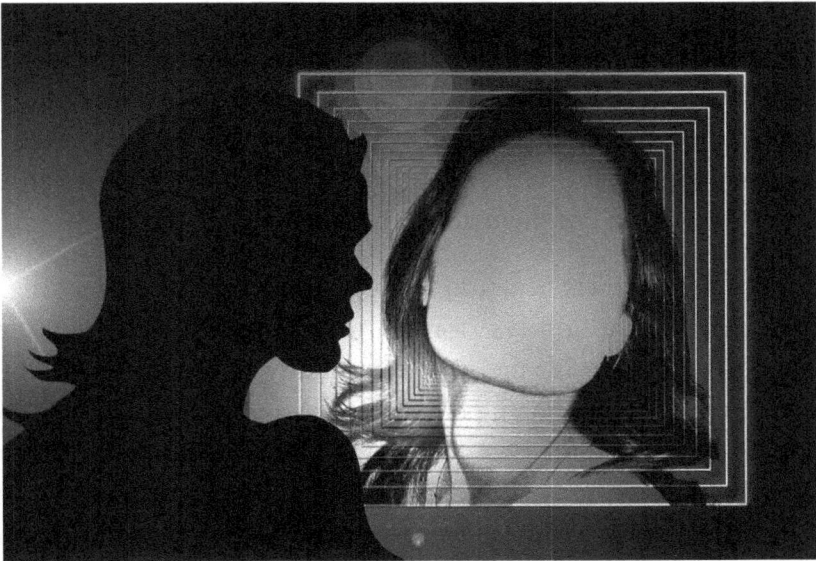

For several years now, the theory of mind control has been about. People were both fascinated and afraid of what would happen if someone could control their minds and make them do things contrary to their will. There are countless conspiracy theories about government leaders and other influential individuals who use their abilities to monitor what small groups of people do. Even some court cases were brought up using the brainwashing excuse as an explanation of why they committed the crime they are accused of. Despite the play-up of mental control depicted in the media and films, little is understood about the various forms of mental control and how each of them functions.

Although many different types of mind control can be used to control the intended victim, the most commonly thought of are five. This involves hypnosis, brainwashing, coercion, persuasion, and deceit. These are all to be discussed in the following.

BRAINWASHING

Brainwashing is the first kind of mind control to be debated. Brainwashing is essentially the process where someone would be convinced to give up convictions they had in the past and take on new principles and ideals. There are many ways this can be achieved, but not all of them are considered evil.

For instance, if you're from an African nation and then moving to America, you are always forced to change your beliefs and principles to fit in with the new community and climate in which you live. On the other hand, people in concentration camps, or when a new dictatorial regime takes over, will also go through the process of brainwashing to convince citizens to obey in peace. Many people misunderstand what brainwashing is about. Many people have more cynical ideas about the procedure, like mind-control systems that are funded by the government and thought to be quickly turned on with a remote control. On the other side of things, some skeptics don't believe brainwashing is possible at all, and whoever says it is has spread lies. The form of brainwashing will probably fall somewhere between these two theories.

During the brainwashing practice, the target can be convinced by a mixture of techniques to change their views about something. In this method, there is not just one technique that can be used, and it can be difficult to bring the practice into a tidy little package. The subject will also be disconnected from all the things they learn.

From there, they are broken down into an emotional state which makes them fragile before new concepts are implemented. As this new knowledge is absorbed by the subject, they will be rewarded for sharing ideas and thoughts that go with these new ideas. This should be used to justify the brainwashing that is taking place is rewarding.

Brainwashing is nothing new to society. For a long time, people have been using such techniques. For example, those who were prisoners of war were sometimes broken down in a historical context, before being convinced to change sides. Some of those most successful cases would result in the inmate becoming a very fervent convert to the new side. In the beginning, such activities were very new and would always be applied based on who was in command. The concept of brainwashing was developed over time, and a few more methods were added to make the practice more widespread. The newer techniques will focus on the field of psychology because many of those concepts were used to show how people, by persuasion, could change their minds.

Several steps go along with the process of brainwashing. It's not something that can happen to you just as you walk down the street and talk to someone you just met. First of all, one of the main demands that come with successful brainwashing is that the subject should be kept in isolation. If the subject is around other people and experiences, they can learn how to behave like an adult, and there will be no brainwashing at all.

They can undergo a process designed to break down their selves if the subject is isolated. They're told all the facts they know are wrong, and they're made to feel like they're wrong with everything they do. The subject will feel like they're bad after months of going through all of this and will be overwhelmed by the guilt. Once they have reached this point, the manipulator will begin to lead them to the desired new system of beliefs and identity. The subject would be led to believe that all of the new opinions are their own, and therefore, they are more likely to last. The entire brainwashing cycle can take months or even years or complete. It's not something that's going to happen in just a conversation, and it won't be able to happen outside of detention camps and a few isolated situations for the most part.

For the most part, when someone is simply trying to convince othersof a different point of view, those are people who experience brainwashing. For example, if you're in an argument with a friend, and they're telling you their ideas make sense, you've technically been through brainwashing. Sure, it may not be bad, and you might objectively think about it all, but you were also persuaded to alter previously held convictions. It is unlikely that someone undergoes real brainwashing where they would have changed their whole belief system. It will usually occur during the process of getting around to a new point of view, irrespective of whether or not the tactics used were forceful.

HYPNOSIS

The next, well-known form of mind control is hypnosis. The several meanings of what hypnosis is are different. Hypnosis is a mutual activity, according to the American Psychological Association, in which the hypnotist will provide suggestions that the patient will respond to. Many people have become familiar with hypnosis techniques thanks to popular performances in which participants are told to perform ridiculous or unusual tasks. Another form of hypnosis that is gaining in popularity is the type that uses this practice for its therapeutic and medical advantages, especially when it comes to reducing anxiety and pain. In some cases, hypnosis has been able to reduce dementia symptoms in a few patients. There are, as you can see, several different explanations that can be used for hypnosis. If the hypnotist will give solutions that may be detrimental or alter the way the client behaves in their situation, that is the point where it starts to become mind control.

When most people hear about hypnosis, they think of a person on stage who swings a watch back and forth to put the participant in a trance. If you go to a stage show for amusement, you might picture some of the absurd actions performed by the participants in your mind. Those who are going through what is considered to be real hypnosis are going through a very different process. "The individual is not hypnotized by the hypnotist. The hypnotist then acts as a sort of coach or mentor whose task is to help the person become hypnotized,"John Kihlstrom said. This means the hypnotist is trying to bring the client into a relaxed state of mind, so they are more open to suggestions offered.

Most of the hypnosis sufferers claim they are in a kind of sleeplike dream state. Notwithstanding these feelings, while the patient is in a state under hypnosis, it includes vivid hallucinations, increased suggestibility, and concentrated attention. This new condition makes them more responsive to suggestions offered by the hypnotist. The effects that hypnosis can have on subjects are difficult to describe, since the experiences can differ quite a bit for each person who undergoes it. Some participants will describe the feeling as though they are disconnected from the whole process, some will feel highly comfortable during the hypnosis, and others will even believe like their acts will take place beyond their conscious choices. On the other hand, individuals will claim to be fully aware of their surroundings and will even be able to conduct conversations during their hypnotic state.

Several studies done by Ernest Hilgard show that hypnosis can be used to alter the beliefs of the subject. Hilgard's experiment included a warning to the subject that they should not experience any pain in their head. The subject had their arm stuck in some ice water after they were told this. Those who did this experiment and did not get hypnotized had to take their arms out of the water in just a few seconds because they felt pain. Many who had been hypnotized could leave their arms in the water without experiencing any pain for a few minutes. Though more research is required, this study shows how powerful mind control can be when using the technique of hypnosis.

There are several different uses of hypnosis illustrated by studies that include:

Treatment of chronic pain like the one associated with rheumatoid arthritis. Treatment and avoidance of the suffering that comes from childbirth.

Reducing the symptoms related to dementia.

Since using hypnotherapy, some ADHD patients have reported a reduction in their symptoms.

To reduce cases of vomiting and nausea in patients going through chemotherapy.

Pain control during a dental procedure. Eliminating and reducing skin disorders, such as psoriasis and warts, alleviating symptoms linked to Irritable Bowel Syndrome.

These are only a few of the uses for which hypnosis has become popular. While many people believe that using hypnosis is used to manipulate the subject and make it perform cruel actions or reject their values, the most popular applications are those to enhance individuals' safety.

Most experts believe that hypnosis as a method of mind control is not a fact. Although it may be possible to convince the mind to make a few changes in the subject's behavior, it is impossible that the subject will change their whole belief system even by this process. Many of the people who are trained in this field would use it to assist the subject in handling self-improvement and discomfort rather than attempting to take over their minds.

MANIPULATION

Manipulation is another type of mind control which can be used in various ways to decide how the person thinks. Manipulation is referred to in this guidebook as psychological manipulation. It is a sort of social power that serves to alter other people's actions or understanding. It is done using methods that are hostile, insulting, and underhanded. This form of mind control is used, often to the detriment of others, to advance the one controlling desires. The approaches employed are also perceived as manipulative, devious, coercive, and exploitative. Most people can understand when controlled or others controlled around them, but they don't identify that as a form of mind control. It can also be a difficult form of mind control to resist as the coercion generally takes place between the subject and someone they know well. Manipulation leaves the subject feeling as if they have no choice. They would have been fed lies or half-truths outright, and they would not know the full severity of the case until it was too late. When they find out ahead of time about the situation, the manipulator would be able to threaten and use the subject to achieve the final target. By fact, the subject gets lost, and the manipulator will have worked it out in such a way that they won't fall into trouble, the subject will take the blame or get hurt when it comes to it, and the manipulator can make it to their final target.

The worst thing about this is that the manipulator is unable to sense their subject's needs or any other person's needs; they won't know whether the subject gets harmed in the process and if it's emotional or physical damage. Although the subject will be involved emotionally in the situation, the manipulator will be able to walk away (as long as they achieve their ultimate goal) without feeling any guilt or regret for what happened along the way. This can be a dangerous type of mind control because the manipulator will be an expert at it, capable of blackmailing, threatening, and doing whatever else is needed; often, they will even be able to turn it around, so the target feels like they're going insane.

PERSUASION

Persuasion is another type of mind controlthatacts to manipulate the subject's actions, emotions, thoughts, attitudes, and beliefs. There are many different reasons why persuasion could be used in everyday life, and it's often a necessary form of communication to get people on the same page with different ideas. For business, for example, the persuasion mechanism can be used to shift the attitude of a person about anything, such as, a concept, or event that is happening. During the process, either written or spoken words are used to pass reasoning, feelings, or information on to the other person. Convincing another may be used to satisfy a personal gain. This may include encouraging trials, when delivering a sales pitch, or during an election campaign. Although none of these are considered negative or bad, they are all used to convince the listener to act or think in some way. One definition of persuasion is that one uses their own personal or professional power to alter others' attitudes or behaviors. There are also many different forms of persuasion known; the process of changing beliefs or attitudes by appealing to reason and reasoning is known as systemic persuasion; the process of changing beliefs and attitudes by appealing to feelings or behaviors is known as heuristic persuasion.

Persuasion is a form of control of the mind that is used all the time in society. When you talk about politics to someone, you can try to convince them to think the same way you do. If you listen to a political advertisement, you are motivated to vote in one direction or another. If anyone wants to sell you a new product, there's a lot of persuasion going on there. This form of mind control is so widespread that most people don't even know it's happening to them. The problem will occur when someone takes the time to convince you to believe in beliefs and principles that do not suit your belief system. There are several different kinds of persuasion on sale. Maybe all of them have negative intent, but they will all try to get the target to change their minds about something. When a political candidate appears on television on election day, they try to get the subject, or the voter, to vote on the ballot a certain way. The company that produced the advertising is trying to get the audience to purchase that product when you see a commercial on television or online. These are all forms of persuasion bent on trying to get the target to change the way they think.

DECEPTION

Finally, deception is often considered a form of mind control because of its potential effect on the subject. Deception is used to spread assumptions about events and things in the subject's life which are not real, regardless of whether they are full lies or just partial lies. Deception may include several different items like hand sleight, concealment, disguise, and diversion. This kind of mind control is dangerous because the subject sometimes does not know that there is any kind of mind control at all. We are persuaded that when the complete opposite is right, one thing is real. It can become dangerous when the deception hides details that would keep the subject secure. Often during relationships, deception is seen and will usually lead to feelings of distrust and betrayal between the two partners. There has been a violation of the relationship rules when deceit happens, and it may make it impossible for the partner to trust the other for a long time. It can be particularly dangerous because most people are used to trusting those around them, especially partners and friends, and often expect them to be true to them. When they find out they're being misled by someone they're close to, they may have problems with trusting people, and they won't have the sense of security they're used to.

Deception can trigger several problems in a relationship, or the manipulator and subject. Once they find out about the deception, the subject will have a lot of issues trusting the manipulator in the future. There will be occasions where the lie is made to help the partnership out. This may involve things like not asking a partner when someone says they mean something. Other times the deception is of a more spiteful or harmful nature, such as when the manipulator hides important information from the subject or even deceives the person as to who they are. All people believe that deceit is unethical and should not be performed, no matter what form of deceit is deployed.

Chapter 3:

How to Read People

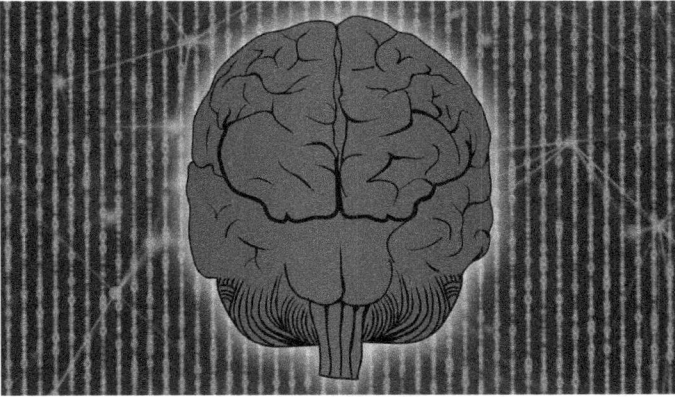

What you say communicates only half of what people hear. 40-50% of the message you send comes from your body language. Since the last century, we have made a lot of progress in understanding the thousands of non-verbal communication meanings. Here are some of the most important findings:

FACIAL EXPRESSIONS

How good are you at reading facial expressions? There are currently online tests that tell you whether you're good at reading facial expressions or not. Some tests like Reading the Mind in the Eyes Test checks to see whether you can read a person's mind simply by looking at their eyes. If you're interested in taking the test yourself, check the website: socialintelligence.labinthewild.org/mite. See how well you fare and then just come back to this book if you want. For purposes of improving communication, we're going to include all the elements that are included in reading facial expressions, which involve the eyes, eyebrows, lips, nose, and even the wrinkles around the eyes and mouth.

PUPIL

There is practically no way to fake the movement of the pupils when reading facial expressions. The pupils of the eye contract and expand without any sort of control on the part of a person. Typically, the pupils will expand when a person is interested and contract when they're not.

BLINKING MOTION

The eyes typically blink six to ten times per minute. When a person looks at something they find interesting, however, that blinking rate slows down drastically. It's therefore a great indicator when someone finds something interesting or attractive. It's often used as a sign of flirting or interest in a romantic setting. In an office or social setting, unblinking eyes could be a signal that a person is very interested in what you have to say and listening to you throughout.

RAISING THE HEAD

Raising the head from a lowered position is a sign of captured interest. Think of a student who's looking down during an exam who suddenly raises their head when they hear something important. This is the kind of movement that we are trying to describe in this situation.

HEAD TILT

A head tilt usually starts from a normal position of the head and then juts out at an angle. This is what makes it different from the motion of raising your head from a lowered position. A head tilt also indicates interest, usually towards the person or activity where it happens to be tilted too. When combined with facial expressions like a narrowing of the eyebrows, it can be a sign of confusion, curiosity, questioning, or uncertainty. A head that's tilted backward may be a sign of suspicion.

Of course, let's not forget the typical head gestures that mean practically the same for everyone. These are:

NODDING

Usually signifies agreement.

SHAKING THE HEAD

Usually signifies disagreement. What's important about these gestures is that people are often conscious of doing this. Hence, it can be easily controlled by them, depending on the situation. Some can stop the motion entirely while others turn it into very subtle gestures so that it would be very difficult to notice.

HANDS, ARMS, AND GESTURES

SHRUG

A shrug is composed of multiple gestures which include exposed palms, hunched shoulders, and raised brows. It's a universal sign that indicates a lack of knowledge or uncertainty over a particular activity. It can often be translated as a sign that the other person doesn't know what you're saying or doesn't understand what you're trying to convey.

CLENCHED HANDS

Clenched hands are a sign of repression. You're trying to prevent the burst of emotions like anger or frustration. It's a self-containment mechanism often used by people who don't want to do or say something out of order. In some cases, you can read this gesture as a sign that someone has a closed mind on what you're trying to say. In the alternative, open and relaxed hands are a sign of comfort and show a positive attitude with a mind welcome to new ideas.

HAND WRINGING

This is often interpreted as a sign of anxiety or nervousness. Playing with something in your hands also has the same interpretation.

HANDSHAKE

You have to be careful with handshakes as this can tell so much about a person and vice versa. I'm sure you've managed to have presumptions of people simply because of the way they shook your hand.

The best handshake is often considered to be a firm, dry grip, that's quick but not too long. It shouldn't be too tight as to cause pain, but it should be strong enough to signify competence on the part of the person shaking their hand.

My advice is you practice your handshake with another person to help you decide on the best pressure to use when greeting someone this way. Note though—not all cultures accept handshakes as a viable way of greeting others. For example, people in India or those who practice the Muslim faith do not approve of handshakes as a way of greeting between men and women.

COVERING THE MOUTH

Doing this is often shown as a sign of repression, like a person wanted to say something but decided against it at the last minute. Some people use this gesture as a way to show thinking or a thought process.

BODY POSTURE AND MOVEMENT

You've probably noticed that reading body language involves paying attention to different parts of the body all at once. Some gestures are centered in just one area, like the face, and therefore are slightly easier than others. Some gestures, however, are scattered all over the body, which means that different parts are moving all at once. This makes it tougher to do a reading, but you'll find that with practice, the whole thing becomes easier.

Body posture and movement is a big predictor of a person's thoughts and emotions.

The general position of the chest, shoulders, legs, and so on will tell you if a person is aggressive, afraid, unsure, excited, and so on. Here are some of the typical changes in the body and what they indicate:

A PUMPED-OUT CHEST IS A SIGN OF POWER AND DOMINANCE

Typically, when the chest is spread out, the shoulders are also stretched into a straight line, pushing the chest forward and making the person appear bigger. Combined with hands placed on the hips and this can be dubbed as the "Superman" pose which makes a person appear bigger and occupy more space. This is often seen as a sign of confidence and dominance.

You'll notice many animals in the wild, when protecting their territory or trying to attract a mate, tend to make their bodies appear bigger so that they'll be easily noticed.

Men and women do the same thing and often for the same reasons.

TOUCHING THE CHEST CAN ALSO BE A SIGN OF SINCERITY

You'll notice how people do this when they're trying to apologize or communicate how bad they feel or their condolences to another person.

Scratching or touching the chest can also be a sign of discomfort.

BREATHING

Breathing can tell you a lot about what a person feels. You've probably noticed this already, not just in other people but also in yourself. For example, you might hold your breath when excited or take short and shallow breaths when scared. Typically, deep and even breaths are indicative of relaxation, such as when you're sleeping or when you're sitting down watching a relaxing movie. Excessive, shallow, or holding your breath, on the other hand, can be a sign of emotional turmoil. According to experts, mirroring a person's breathing pattern can also help forge a connection of mutual understanding between the two of you. Being able to match someone's breathing pattern essentially allows you to create a sense of normalcy in the situation, thereby pulling them into a sense of relaxation. Of course, this takes some skill to do, especially if the situation is nerve-wracking. At the very least, being able to identify nervous breathing patterns can help you adjust your stance to make the other person feel comfortable—all without a word said to each other.

READING LIES IN PEOPLE

One of the most valuable skills when reading people is being able to tell when they're lying. Admit it—you've always wanted to know when someone is lying to you, and that's perfectly okay. Studies show that when lying, some people have specific "tells," such as scratching their nose or brushing their hair with their fingers. People who play poker often use these "tells" to see if they should match the other person's bet and whether it would be worth the trouble.

One thing I want to remind you of is that reading lies in a person is not an exact science. People's actions when lying can vary, which is why familiarity is important. The longer you know a person, the more accurate your prediction will be about the truthfulness of what they're saying.

So, that being the case, here are the typical signs of lying according to experts.

Understanding a Baseline

One thing I want you to remember is that when reading body language, there's usually a "baseline" that allows you to start somewhere. A baseline is simply the "normal" way in which a person acts when around people. Hence, if a person is being truthful and confident in their surroundings, how exactly do they act? Knowing a person's baseline lets you know when they're acting out of character. Sure, you can walk into a room full of strangers and do a casual "read" of the room, but reading people close to you is often easier as you've known them for a longer period. You have a point of reference, to put it simply.

Hand Movements

People lying tend to use gestures, but they do it after speaking. Typically, you'd find people gesturing while talking because that is a natural part of the process.

Their body is working with the mind in telling a story or conveying a message. In contrast, a person who is lying is focusing too much on making up the story that the body fails to catch up.

Hence, they make up the lie first and then perform the gestures to emphasize their point. Also, take note that gestures of people who are lying often involve both hands as opposed to truthful people who only use one hand. This was noted after a 2015 study about people testifying in court cases.

ITCHING AND FIDGETING

There's a popular belief that when a person lies, they tend to scratch their nose. This isn't true 100% of the time—but it does bear noting in many cases. It's fairly normal for people to have an itching sensation or fidget in their seat when they're uncomfortable; the body naturally looks for a way to distract itself. Also note that when lying, people are often nervous about what they're saying, which causes the autonomic nervous system to fluctuate, thus, creating that tingling sensation all over the body. It's a lot like the nerves you get when you sit close to someone you like during those younger days.

FACIAL EXPRESSIONS

Of course, let us not forget how the face itself can signify when someone is lying. The eyes in particular can tell you so much depending on when a person chooses to look at you and when they choose to look away. Looking too much or not looking at all can be indicative of lying. Some people prefer to meet your gaze when lying because they "think" this will impress upon you their sincerity. Non-experienced liars tend to look away when uttering a lie.

CHANGE IN COMPLEXION

This one's pretty obvious, as you read about it every day or see it as it happens every day. People blush, people become red, and people become pale depending on the circumstances. People tend to become pale when they're nervous or when they're afraid of something. When the skin turns a shade of red, however, that's indicative of anger or perhaps even excitement, like when a teenager typically blushes when sitting beside their crush.

SWEAT IN THE T ZONE

This is something you have to watch out for when wondering if a person is lying to you or not. The T Zone covers the area of the nose and across the forehead and then down to your mouth. Sweating is fairly common in this area if a person is lying, especially if they're nervous about it.

TONE OF VOICE

We're trying to focus on nonverbal communication here, but the tone of voice is still a strong indicator, even with the absence of the words themselves. High-pitched voices tend to come out of nervous people as the vocal cords tighten, making it hard to push out the particular words. There can also be a croak, a stutter, or some broken words coming out of a nervous individual. Some people clear their throat to help improve their speech, which is also indicative of nervousness. In contrast, a loud and booming voice can be a sign of confidence or anger, depending on the situation. A sudden change in the volume can also be defensive in people, especially when confronted with possible mistakes.

THE MOUTH

Playing with the lips, such as rolling them back until they almost disappear, is another good indicator.

It's typically a sign of lying by omission as people physically try to hold back a word or a thought by pulling in their lips.

If it goes the other way, however, it can be a sign of resistance or when a person doesn't want to talk about something.

THE WORDS THEMSELVES

Again, we're trying to focus on the nonverbal way of communicating, but I still want to cover all bases. After all, experienced liars can easily control their body language to match the situation. Hence, you still have to listen to the words themselves as they can indicate when a person is trying too hard to convince you of their truthfulness. Some common phrases used by liars include:

"Honestly…"

"Let me tell you the truth…"

"Uh…"

"Like…"

"Um…"

Chapter 4:

Users of Dark Psychology

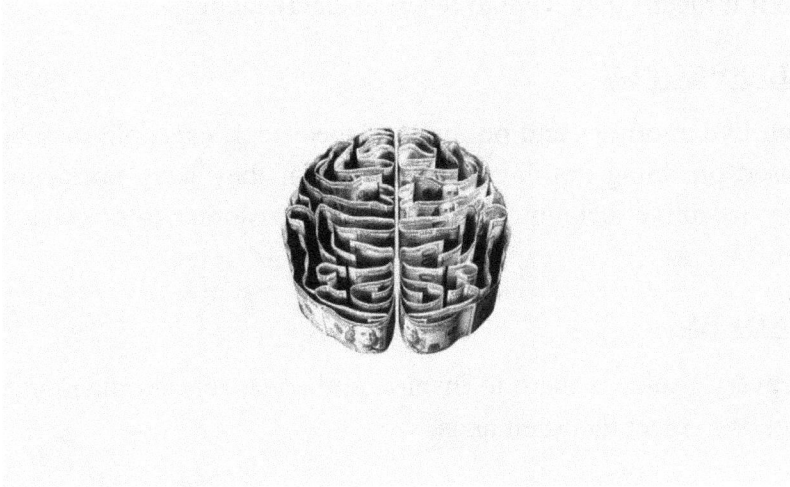

WHO USES DARK PSYCHOLOGY THESE DAYS?

ATTORNEYS

Many attorneys focus so attentively on winning their case that they turn to use techniques of dark manipulation to get the outcome they seek.

THE SELFISH PEOPLE

Someone with a secret agenda that favors itself before anyone can return to those dark, deceptive tactics if the result is a win for them.

POLITICIANS

To get the votes they need to get the people to vote in the way they want them, politicians are guilty of using dark methods of manipulation as a means of serving their purpose.

LAWYERS

Some lawyers will stop at nothing if it means winning their case, even if it means they have to resort to shady tactics.

SALESPEOPLE

Much like attorneys and politicians, specific salespeople may be so focused on doing nothing but selling that they have no shame in using deceptive techniques to convince a customer to do what they want.

LEADERS

Not every leader is there to inspire, and some rely on manipulation to get us to meet their demands.

PUBLIC SPEAKERS

Not all public speakers can be trusted, and there are some out there whowill resort to bribery if it means selling more goods to do so.

Many speakers use dark strategies to heighten the audience's emotional state of realizing it leads to more products being sold at the back of the room.

These are just a few of the many instances of people out there who would turn to the more malevolent side of the continuum of human nature, and often for the benefit of no one else but their own.

THE TRIAD OF DARK PSYCHOLOGY

Just when you felt the deceit was bad enough, an even darker side of psychology arrives here, known as the Dark Triad. The triad consists of three very distinct but interrelated forms of personality, namely narcissism, psychopathy, and Machiavellianism. Why is the Dark Triad, or the darker side of human psychology, called these three? It is because these three terms define the very tactics that some people resort to getting what they want-manipulation, persuasion, and deception. Yes, the term Dark Triad has a sinister ring to it, and it's a term that many psychologists and criminologists use as a defining predictor that signals an individual's criminal behavior. Let's look at the three personality characteristics that make up this trifecta more closely:

NARCISSISM

The word comes from the Greek mythology of Narcissus, the hunter who fell in love with his reflection when he saw it in a pool of water where he drowned. He was so consumed by himself that he could not concentrate on anything else. Those with characteristics of narcissistic personality also show signs that include being boastful, greedy, and rude, caring more for themselves and nothing else. Also, narcissistic individuals lack empathy and are highly sensitive (one may even say hypersensitive) to any sort of criticism, since they cannot bear the incomplete or false thought.

MACHIAVELLIANISM

This word comes from the famous diplomat and politician Niccolò Machiavelli who lived in Italy in the 16th century. Machiavelli became famous with the publication of his book, The Prince, in 1513. This publication has been interpreted as the recognition by Machiavelli of the deception and ruse that takes place in diplomacy. Those who tend to exhibit Machiavellianistic tendencies are often only concerned with their self-interest and are manipulative and duplicate. Some people lack both morals and conscience, so they're not into anything else but what's going to help them.

PSYCHOPATHY

Antisocial behavior, manipulative, aggressive, violent, lack of guilt, or empathy are characteristics associated with a psychopathic character. Psychopathic and being a psychopath are two very different features, the latter generally associated with or explicitly associated with crime.

THE MANIPULATOR

The term manipulative is likely to affect individuals of all social origins. The typical manipulator usually has a perverse psychological structure of the psychopathic type; he can appear as friendly or not, even as a victim. It seems that each one is more or less manipulative in the course of his life.

According to these definitions, different types of manipulators can be distinguished: those who use others without remorse, with a narcissistic goal of power, financial scam, or with malicious intent. They can rely on lies or seduction, even coercion by threat of force, or destabilize their victim by double oppression. Psychic manipulation can be one of the tools of certain forms of torture.

It can be behavior understood as deviant or perverse, a personality disorder whose causes go back to childhood or the manipulator's education, such as if his parents or educators have manipulated him. Psychologists are frequently confronted with manipulative behavior in systems such as family or socio-professional.

Mental manipulation could be a certain form of selfishness. Often the manipulator demands socially acceptable behavior from others without adapting themselves. He appropriates the ideas of another, conversely trying to make someone else take his responsibilities. The arguments of a manipulator always seem, at first glance, logical and moral. Usually, he uses pretexts such as the norm, the "good behavior" that must be observed in society or the group, knowing how to use the weaknesses of others, for example making them feel ridiculous, guilty, or hurt in their modesty, which places them in a mental situation favorable to manipulation.

A SADIST

A professional sadist can so deliberately set these conditions up that it is impossible to prove that they were involved in the guilty party. What makes it far worse is that they will never be held responsible or feel any sort of regret for the harm they caused. People can also be hesitant to assume that the sadist's charming and likable personalities are behind the chaos. A sadist will attempt to harm someone else intentionally because they believe that doing so will benefit them. They may resort to such underhanded tactics if they feel envious or threatened by others or even if they perceive someone else as weaker and less likely to retaliate against them. In some instances, it might not be obvious why the sadist opted to conduct a victim attack. We don't often think-or want to believe-that the sadist might exist within our immediate circle of connections, but they do, and they could be your parents, siblings, extended family members, spouse, friends, and the people with whom you work.

THE MANIPULATOR IN A RELATIONSHIP

One of the worst sinking feeling you might feel is knowing that all this time, your partner, the person you love and who supposedly loves you, turns out to be using you to their advantage. A partnership is supposed to be the one place we believe we can get the sincere inside support, love, dedication, and care we all yearn for. In return, to be wholeheartedly loved and respected. Sadly, there are those out there who have had their hearts broken because they know there's not just something dishonest about their partner, but they have manipulated their strings like a puppet all along.

We all have particular aspirations and romantic ideas of what we think love is due to the way in which love is portrayed in society through the films we watch, articles we read, and social media posts we scroll through almost every day. When we see on-screen jealousy, we believe it's a sign of intense love because the two people in the film are afraid to lose their loved one to another. The popular literature and Twilight movies lead us to believe that true love and relationships are about obsession. That love is an omnipresent emotion. That when there are two people in love, nothing else matters, and there are no boundaries. This romanticized notion blinds us to the fact that this isn't what life is at all, and that kind of love occurs only in movies and between the pages of books because they make for a good storyline. Such behavior is an indication of manipulation in real life. It is not love to be controlling, it is manipulation. It is not being passionate being obsessed, and it is manipulative.

On some level, we know that we should be able to recognize in a relationship the signs of an abusive partner. We know we can, but it is easier said than done. When we love, we prefer to blind ourselves to a fault with our mate. We are making excuses for the actions that should set off warning bells in our heads as we try to avoid facing the facts. We don't want our hearts to be broken that way, and we're trying to convince ourselves they aren't really like that at all. There is cause for concern when a relationship escalates from controlling to being purely abusive but being in a manipulative relationship can also be harmful and damaging.

Getting in a manipulative relationship can be as detrimental to you both physically and psychologically. Manipulative partners will try to dominate you, minimizing your freedom. They try to manipulate every decision you make, belittle you, and destroy your self-esteem so that you begin to doubt yourself and think you are the "lucky" one, and no one can possibly love you as much. They make you scared of losing this relationship and make you scared to enter into any future relationships because this experience has traumatized you from getting into another manipulative relationship. Being in a manipulative relationship will leave you with emotional wounds and scars that, if they ever do, will take a very, very long time to heal.

The more common signs you're in a manipulative relationship is when your partner continually pressures you to look or act in a way that they only approve of or decide who you can and can't spend your time with. The love and support that would come from genuine relationships is not something you will note when you're in a relationship with manipulators. Lying to try to manipulate you and the situation in their favor, when your partner is a manipulative person, is something that will be a regular occurrence in your relationship, and these are the signs to look out for:

- Lying to make you feel guilty about spending time with others—Because the manipulator needs to be in charge, they will try to cut you off as far as possible from your support network by trying to minimize the amount of time you spend with your family and friends.

- They lie and criticize— When you're with someone manipulative, every little thing you do is subject to criticism. The worst part of all this is that they lie so convincingly when they say they do it because "they love you" or "it's for your good". They'll continually criticize just about everything you're doing, the longer you remain in a relationship with them.

- You may be the most trustworthy and truthful person, but a manipulator will make you feel different. They are still individuals in their own right, as deeply in love as two people are, and all have the right to privacy.

- Manipulators may demand access to your passwords, social media accounts, and even more private information by spinning some tale about how they're "fearing" you might break their hearts by cheating on them.

- They're talking a lot about "protecting you," which, of course, is just another lie by the manipulator. They're not protecting you; they're not even thinking about it, because all they care about is their self-interest. Deep down, who wouldn't love the idea that there's somebody out there who loves them enough to protect them from the big evil world? That person exists, alas not with a manipulator. There's a natural desire to protect when you love someone and to keep them from feeling hurt.

- They provoke you with lies — Sometimes a manipulator might resort to provoking you into an argument by lying and exaggerating, blowing things out of proportion just because they know that when they do, and they push your buttons.

- Twisting lies with even more lies — Manipulators will spin lies almost as intricately as spinning their website. They will lie, twist those lies, and then twist those lies even more until you don't know what is real and what isn't. Twisting the truth and distorting them, tangling lies on top of more lies is the manipulator's favorite technique to confuse and frustrate you.

Chapter 5:

Behaviors Exhibited by Attackers

EMOTIONAL INTELLIGENCE AND MANIPULATION

The term emotional intelligence was first invented in the 1960s and has become common over the years.

However, the concept behind the term has been around for decades. In simple terms, emotional intelligence is the ability of a person to recognize and understand emotions, then using this information to make decisions.

Like any other skill, emotional intelligence is a skill we can cultivate, sharpen, and enhance. It is important to note that although emotional intelligence is a good skill, one can use it either for good or bad.

Once a person understands the power of emotions, he or she can use it ethically or unethically.

The last thing that we want is having someone manipulating our emotions, whether it is a friend, colleague, or politician.

There are some ways through which a master manipulator can use emotional intelligence against you. Please note that not everyone who has the characteristics listed below and used the said skill has selfish intentions. Some people practice them with no intended harm. Nonetheless, having an increased awareness of these behaviors will empower you to deal with manipulators strategically and sharpen your intelligence quotient in the process.

MANIPULATORS PLAY ON FEAR

The majority of manipulators will overemphasize specific points and exaggerate facts to make you scared and have you acting as they want.

The way to identify this play is by looking out for statements that imply you are not strong or courageous enough or that if you miss out on a particular thing, you are a loser.

MANIPULATORS DECEIVE

Everybody values honesty and transparency, thus, will want to avoid deceivers. Manipulators understand this concept and are very cunning when lying.

They twist the facts or try to show you only the side of the story that benefits them. For instance, a work colleague can spread some unconfirmed rumor to gain an upper hand.

47

MANIPULATORS TAKE ADVANTAGE OF YOUR HAPPINESS

Have you noticed that you are more likely to say yes to anything when you are happy or in a good mood? When we are happy, we tend to jump on opportunities that look good even before we think things through. Master manipulators have this knowledge, thus, will take advantage of the moods. To manage this emotional opportunity and avoid manipulation, work to improve awareness of your emotions, both positive and negative. strive to strike a balance between logic and emotions When making decisions.

MANIPULATORS TAKE ADVANTAGE OF RECIPROCITY

Do you know that feeling you get when you owe someone a favor especially if they helped you at one point? That feeling of debt makes one vulnerable. It is hard to say no to a manipulator if you owe them something. Most of the manipulators will attempt to butter and flatter you with small favors then ask for a big one in return.

As much as giving brings more joy than receiving, it is more important to know your limits.

Do not be afraid to say no, even if you owe someone a favor.

MANIPULATORS PUSH FOR A HOME-COURT ADVANTAGE

It is very easy to convince a person when you are in a familiar place. As such, a manipulator will push you towards meeting you in a place he or she is familiar with while you are not. Ownership gives power and comfort, thus, a place like home or the office will give the manipulator some authority. You will have to make requests for meeting in a neutral place where familiarity and ownership are diluted to disarm the manipulator.

THE MANIPULATOR WILL ASK A LOT OF QUESTIONS

Naturally, it is easy to talk about oneself. Master manipulators know this; thus, they take advantage to ask some probing questions.

Their agendas are hidden but they seek to discover your weaknesses or other information they can hold against you.

Of course, it would be unfair for you to assume that everyone has wrong motives because there are a few people who genuinely seek to know you better. However, it is okay to question people, especially those who reveal nothing about themselves.

THE MANIPULATOR WILL SPEAK QUICKLY

To manipulate you through your emotions, the manipulator will speak quickly and sometimes use jargon and special vocabulary.

This will give them an advantage because you will not have enough time to think. For you to counter this form of manipulation, do not feel afraid to ask for some time to process what the person said. Also, make a point of asking the person to repeat any unclear statements. To gain control of a conversation, repeat the points the other person makes in your own words, and let them sink in.

THE DISPLAY OF NEGATIVE EMOTIONS

Some manipulators will use voice tones to control your emotions. The most commonly used tone and body language by manipulators are negative. For instance, basketball coaches (they use manipulation for positive purposes) are masters at raising their voices and using strong body language to manipulate the emotions of the players. To avoid such manipulation, you should practice pausing. It involves taking a break from the conversation orsituation and having some time to think before reacting. You may walk away for some minutes to get a grip on your own emotions.

MANIPULATORS LIMIT YOUR TIME TO ACT

Every manipulator wants to win. They may do this by ensuring that you do not have enough time to think. For instance, an individual may force you to make a serious decision in an unreasonably limited amount of time.

He or she will try to steer your thoughts to their advantage. You will not have enough time to weigh the consequences. To avoid a situation where you give in without thought, do not be in a rush to submit. Ensure that the demand is reasonable. Take the pause, ask for some time, and if the person does not allow you to think, walk away. You will be happier looking for whatever you need elsewhere.

THE SILENT TREATMENT

To avoid being a victim of manipulation through silent treatment, give people deadlines, and do not allow them to intimidate you.

For instance, after attempting to communicate to a reasonable degree, let go of the matter and let the other person reach out.

Manipulators will work to increase their emotional awareness to have an upper hand on others. A large number of people are learning how to be emotionally intelligent.

CHARACTERISTICS OF MANIPULATORS

USE OF LANGUAGE

We have shown how powerful language can bea prime tool of persuasion. There is more to the manipulative controller though, than mere words. They will use tactics that mislead and unbalance their target's inner thoughts. We now understand that through language, they will:

Use mistruths to mislead and confuse their target's normal thinking pattern.

Force their target to decide the speed, so they don't have time to analyze and think.

Overwhelmingly talk to their target, making them feel small.

Criticize their target's judgment so they begin to lose their self-esteem.

Raise the tone of their voice and not be afraid to use aggressive body language.

Ignore their target's needs, as they are only interested in getting what they want and at any cost.

INVASION OF PERSONAL SPACE

Most of us set boundaries around ourselves without realizing we are doing so. It is a kind of unspoken rule to protect our own private space, such as not sitting so close that you are touching another person, especially a stranger. A manipulative character cares nothing about overstepping such boundaries. Whether this is because they do not understand, or they do not care is unclear. Initially, they are unlikely to invade their target's personal space. They will seek to build up a good rapport first. This shows that they do understand boundaries because once they gain the confidence of their target, they will then ignore them.

FODDER FOR THOUGHT

Manipulators tend to be very egocentric, with limited social skills. Their only concern is for themselves. Everything they do in life will be concerning how it affects them, not how their actions affect others. Does this mean that they have a psychopathic disorder?

CREATING RIVALRY

Another tactic of the controlling manipulator is backstabbing. They may tell you how great a person you are to your face, making themselves look good. Behind your back, they are busy spreading malicious gossip and untruths about you. This is a classic trait of a controlling manipulator as it creates a rivalry between people. Then, they can pick sides that will make them look favorable, particularly to their target. It can act as the first stage of getting close to their target. Once bonded, they can start to build up trust, making it easier to manipulate the target in the future. If you recognize a backstabber, keep them at a distance. Their agenda is selfish, so it is better not to let them into your personal life. There is no point treating them as they treat you as revenge. It will turn out to be exhausting playing them at their own game. If they know that you are onto them, they may attempt to lure you back with praise, remember that it is false.

DOMINEERING PERSONALITY

It is unlikely that a manipulative person will outwardly show any form of weakness. An important part of their facade is to show conviction about their views. They seek to impress, believing they are right about everything. Almost to the point that if they realize they are wrong, they will still argue that they are right. On a one-to-one level, that invariably means that your position is always wrong.

PASSIVE AGGRESSIVE BEHAVIOR

A common trait of many hard-core manipulators is passive-aggressive behavior. Because they prefer to be popular, they do not wish to be seen as doing anything wrong. Not that a manipulator would ever admit to doing anything wrong. They are experts with facial expressions that are meant to dominate and intimidate. This may include; knitting eyebrows, grinding teeth, and rolling eyes. It may also include noises such as tutting and grunting sounds.

MOODY BLUES

What of the emotional stability of the manipulator? Is it that which makes them behave the way they do? Do they even know what happiness is? The answer to that is most definitely yes, at least to the latter.

Happiness is a tool used initially to help them manipulate, as a happy target is more likely to comply. This, in itself, makes the manipulator happy, or at least in a sense of what they consider happiness. But their joyfulness is a perverted model of what most others consider happiness to be. Their happiness is often built on the foundations of another's misery.

ACCUSING YOUR RIVAL OF WHAT HE IS BLAMING YOU FOR

This is often referred to as the act of pointing to another person's wrongdoing. When enduring an onslaught and experiencing difficulty regarding safeguarding themselves, manipulators tend to reverse the situation. They blame their rivals for committing the exact things that they are being blamed for. *"You state that I don't love you! I think it is you who does not cherish me!"*

APPEALING TO POWER

Numerous individuals are in wonderment of those in power or authority, or those who have status. What's more intriguing is that there are various images to which individuals experience extraordinary dedication.

Remember, those who are easily manipulated admire those who are in power. Moreover, those who are in power are aware of their ability to control others by never criticizing them. Instead, they use complex misleading tactics to maneuver their thoughts and alter their decision-making process.

APPEALING TO ENCOUNTER

Nevertheless, this appeal to experience provides them with an image of someone capable; this may be used to attack their opponent's lack of experience, even though they have limited experiences. You can easily identify this manipulation tactic at times when someone is trying to distort their capabilities about a particular subject.

APPEALING TO FEAR

People have fears. The unscrupulous manipulators realize a reality that individuals will, in general, respond crudely when any of these feelings of dread are enacted. Subsequently, they speak to themselves as being able to ensure individuals against these dangers, even when they are not capable of doing so. This is the same for when we talked about giving the target a glimpse of how their most desired outcome is achievable, without really providing it to them. Nonetheless, some politicians and legislators frequently utilize this methodology to ensure that individuals line up behind administrative experts and do what the legislature – that is, the government officials – need.

APPEALING TO SYMPATHY

Manipulators can depict themselves and their circumstances to the public to make them feel frustrated about their current situation.

Utilization of this ploy empowers the manipulator to gain consideration from those individuals who may be going through the same thing. Nevertheless, appealing to sympathy is a tactic that most politicians would use to redirect the attention of the public to matters that do not affect their demise.

APPEALING TO WELL-KNOWN INTERESTS

Manipulators and tricksters are always mindful as to how they introduce themselves as persons who possess the right qualities and perspectives among the group of spectators, particularly, the sacred beliefs of the crowd. Everybody has a few partialities, and a great many people feel contempt toward a person or thing. Expert manipulators tend to stir up contempt and prejudices among the crowd.

APPEALING TO CONFIDENCE

This technique is firmly identified with the past points; yet it stresses what appears to have breezed through the trial of time. Individuals are regularly oppressed by the social traditions and standards of their way of life, just as social conventions. What is conventional to most tend to appear as if it is the correct decision. It is important to note that manipulators infer how they regard sacred ideologies and beliefs that the group of spectators are familiar with. These individuals suggest that their enemy aims to obliterate the customs, as well as social conventions.

Moreover, they do not stress over whether or not these conventions hurt guiltless individuals. They make the presence of being autonomous in the crowd's perspective; yet it would typically be the exact opposite.

There is a realization that people are generally suspicious of the individuals who conflict with present social standards and built up conventions.

They realize enough to stay away from them. As a result, there is a kind of restriction on how social traditions are unwittingly and carelessly bound.

BEGGING THE INQUIRY

One simple approach to demonstrate a point is to accept it in any case. Think about this model:

"Well, what type of government do you want, a government by liberal do-gooders that can shell out your hard-earned dollars or a governmentcontrolled by business minds that know how to live within a strict budget and generate jobs that put people to work?"

One minor departure from this error has been classified as "question-begging epithets," the utilization of expressions is a prejudgment of an issue by how it is allowed. For instance, "Shall we defend freedom and democracy or cave into terrorism and tyranny?" Through the inquiry along these lines, we abstain from discussing awkward inquiries like: "Yet, would we say we are truly propelling human opportunity? Are we truly democratic or simply expanding our capacity, our control, our predominance, our access to foreign markets?"

Keep in mind that these are statements individuals utilize when bringing about the truth concerning an issue. There is the regular choosing of statements that surmise the accuracy of the situation on a particular issue.

CREATING A FALSE DILEMMA

A genuine problem happens when we are compelled to pick between two similarly unsuitable choices. A false dilemma happens when we are convinced that we have just two, similarly inadmissible decisions, when we truly have multiple potential outcomes accessible to us. Think about the accompanying case:

"Either we will lose the war on terrorism, or we should surrender a portion of our traditional freedoms and rights."

Individuals are frequently prepared to acknowledge a false dilemma since few are agreeable with the complex qualifications. Clearing absolutes is a part of their manipulative tactics. There is a need to have clear and basic decisions.

HEDGING WHAT YOU STATE

Manipulators frequently hole up behind words, declining to submit themselves or give straightforward replies or answers. This enables them to withdraw in times of need. Whenever they are found forgetting data significant to the current situation, they would think of some other reason for not being able to come up with said information. At the end of the day, when forced, they may be able to give in; however, to be an excellent manipulator, you should renege on your missteps, conceal your mistakes, and gatekeep what you state at whatever point conceivable.

OVERSIMPLIFYING THE ISSUE

Since most people are uncomfortable at comprehending profound or unobtrusive contentions, some are fond of oversimplifying the issue to further their potential benefit. *"I couldn't care less what the measurements inform us concerning the purported abuse of detainees; the main problem is whether we will be tough on crime. Spare your compassion toward the criminals' victims, not for the actual criminals."* The reality being overlooked is that the maltreatment of criminals is a crime in itself. Tragically, individuals with an over-simple mindset could not care less about criminal conduct that victimizes criminals.

RAISING ONLY COMPLAINTS

Your adversary is giving valid justifications to acknowledge a contention; however, the truth of the matter is that your mind's made up and nothing can change it. Gifted manipulators would react with objection after objection. As their rivals answer one protest after another, they would proceed again to object and object. The implicit mentality of the manipulator is that *"regardless of what my rival says, I will continue to object because nothing else will convince me otherwise."*

REWRITING HISTORY

The most noticeably awful acts and outrages tend to vanish from chronicled accounts while false dreams can be made to become facts. This phenomenon is often observed with Patriotic History. The composition of a contorted type of history is supported by the adoration of the nation and is regularly defended by the charge of antagonism. The truth of the matter is that our mind is persistently attempting to re-portray occasions of the past to absolve itself and denounce its spoilers. Chronicled composing frequently goes with the same pattern, particularly in the composition of reading material for schools. In this way, in recounting an anecdote about what has happened, those who perform manipulative tactics do not hesitate to contort the past in the manners in which they accept they can pull off. As usual, the manipulator is prepared with self-justifying excuses.

SHIFTING THE BURDEN OF PROOF

This act alludes to when an individual should demonstrate some of his declarations.

A good example would be the instance that happened inside a court. The examiner possesses the obligation to prove guilt past distrust. Furthermore, the defense should not claim the responsibility of having to prove innocence.

Those who are capable of manipulating others do not need to assume the weight of evidence for what they attest to. Along these lines, they harness the right tool in shifting the burden of proof to their rivals.

TALKING IN VAGUE GENERALITIES AND STATEMENTS

It is difficult to refute individuals when they cannot be bound. So, as opposed to concentrating on specifics, those who are capable of manipulating others tend to speak in the most unclear phrases that they can pull off. We have already talked about how certain statements and generalities can put another person in a daze, which makes it easier for them to be manipulated. This misrepresentation is well known for politicians. For instance, *"Overlook what the cowardly liberals say. It's the right time to be tough, to be hard on criminals, to punish terrorists, and be tough on those who disparage our nation."* Manipulators ensure they do not utilize particulars that may make individuals question what they are doing in the first place.

TELLING ENORMOUS FALSEHOODS AND BIG LIES

The majority of the people are liars, even about the little things; yet there is still a reluctance to say things other than the truth. In any case, these individuals realize that if you insist on a lit long enough, numerous individuals will trust you – particularly, on the off chance that you have the tools of mass media to broadcast a particular lie.

Every gifted manipulator is centered around what you can get individuals to accept, not on what is valid or false. They realize that the human personality does not normally look for reality; it looks for solace, security, individual affirmation, and personal stake.

Individuals regularly would prefer not to know the reality, particularly, certainties that are agonizing, that uncover their logical inconsistencies and irregularities, and that uncover what they hate about themselves or even their nation.

Some so many manipulators are exceptionally gifted in telling huge lies and, in this manner, causing those lies to appear valid.

INTIMIDATION

One aspect of manipulation, often used as a last resort, is intimidation and bullying. When everything else has failed, they begin to use threats to get their way. Some though, may use intimidation from the onset. It may be a source of authority. For example, let's take the role of a manipulative boss. You have requested a day off. They don't want to allow your request but have no choice, it is your right. This type of person would want their pound of flesh first. They will set goals for you to reach so it will delay or cancel your request, such as moving project deadlines forward. This way they have their little victory over you.

THE ASSET OF LISTENING

Listening can be perhaps the most important persuasive tactic you have in your tool kit. Listening to your prospect will give you most of the information you need for a successful persuasive conversation. By listening and paying careful attention to the words and body language, your prospect is communicating and by listening carefully for the words they don't say, you'll be able to discern most of what you need.

THE FAVOR OF O SMILE

Your ability to smile is one of the most powerful tools to influence. This is true of influencing yourself or others. We've learned over thousands of years that the smile is a sign of happiness and friendship, so the smile helps to lower our defenses. When individuals smile, dozens of influential processes happen automatically.

GHOSTING YOU

Guys do this a lot, even if it is something as simple as ghosting you, because it trains you to not get used to hearing from him at certain times, and you always have to reach out to see how he is doing and checking to see if he remembers the date that he set for you. They use their profession or their education to delay you finding out the truth or make you feel like they're always the right one.

DEMONIZE YOUR REACTIONS

They tend to demonize your reactions because anytime someone that is manipulating you and they don't want you to be able to express yourself or control the situation, they will make you feel like you are the bad guy for reacting the way that you did to the situation. They will flip the script on you because you didn't agree with their actions.

You might tell him, "Hey, babe, I don't know why you just liked this girl's picture on Instagram. I thought that we agreed that you won't do this. You show me their stuff. It makes me feel embarrassed that my boy is liking the girl's photos and commenting on rubbish on Instagram, and it makes me feel insecure because you are my boyfriend". Then he will say something like, "you are so insecure, it's just Instagram, I can't believe that you are seriously talking to me about a comment that I wrote to a girl. First of all, I don't even know her, and she looks nice. Other guys are commenting on her photos, but why do you care because I'm with you". So, they demonize you and make you feel like the way you feel is not accounted for. They invalidate the way you feel because he doesn't know that girl, and he may even be trying to get to know her.

USING PITY

One of the greatest forms of manipulation is by using pity. Getting pity out of anybody will guilt-trip them, so because they feel bad for you,they will do what you say, hear you out and whatever trash you want to slip.

For instance, if you say, "I just realized that when we were at the get-together, you didn't want to hang out with me. You were just doing your own thing. I don't know everybody there, I felt alone, and I understand that you know everybody, but I didn't feel included." Then he will say something like, "Honey, I'm sorry that you didn't feel included. However, what do you expect me to do, all the people were people that I grew up with. So, I'm sorry that I wasn't holding your hand the entire time, but I did introduce you to some people. You know that I wouldn't do that to you. You know that I am not like that. I was just caught up. Plus, I saw one of my girlfriends from high school and we just started talking. Come on, if you know me, you know that I wouldn't do something like that. I am not like that."

IT MAKES YOU FEEL GUILTY, AND YOU DON'T KNOW WHY

A master of manipulation consistently goes to victimization. They likely have a "wild card trauma," that is, some problematic episodes in their life that they always expose as a justification for what they do incorrectly.

If, for example, you complain to them for their lack of consideration, they respond by saying something like "you get angry because I am not considerate, but I had to put up with a father who abandoned me when I was three years old." Thus, they disarm you with their traumas. Who will be so insensitive as to complain to someone who has such a past? This is their game.

IT THREATENS YOU WITH SUBTLETY

Threatening indirectly is one of the most recurrent tactics among manipulators. They have used it and continue to use it from the great leaders to the small domestic tyrants, passing through seasoned publicists. This tactic consists of anticipating the worst possible outcome as a consequence of any of your behaviors.

"If you keep eating that way, in 6 months, you will be like a whale." They don't want you to eat, and they probably have no arguments to certify what they say, they just want you not to. Maybe they are bothered by how happy you are when you eat ice cream, or they think you spend too much money on food. They do not openly tell you what they believe, but merely announce a hecatomb.

DISQUALIFY WHAT YOU DO THROUGH SARCASM

If there's one thing a master manipulator hates, it's direct communication. "They don't name you a dog, but they offer you a bone," goes the famous saying. They often use sarcasm to ridicule you or downplay the value of your thoughts, feelings, or actions. The manipulator wants others to feel insecure and inferior. An example of this is when they send you a seemingly friendly message, but which contains quite aggressive content: "Maybe if you read a little more, you could have more select friends." Translated means: "You are an uneducated person, and that's why your friends are poor devils."

Sometimes, the manipulator's victim comes to believe that these kinds of insights are ways to help him be better. Nothing is falser. When someone wants to help another, use direct and honest communication. Also, it does not disqualify you but instead gives you a concrete contribution.

HE IS ALMOST ALWAYS CHARMING

Typical handlers know that "the horse is stroked to mount it." They usually start their job by looking cute and enjoyable. They fill you with compliments and show signs of exquisite tastes, super-entertaining conversation, and high "sensitivity" to your expectations.

SET YOURSELF THE JUDGE OF YOUR LIFE

Without knowing how suddenly the master of manipulation becomes a "spiritual guide" for your life. They are incredibly adept at telling others how they should live, even if they do not put into practice all that they proclaim.

They give you advice or expose your great philosophical sayings. They tell you what to do, bit by bit. If it doesn't work out, they blame you. He told you what to do, dare if you did not follow precisely the instructions that he so generously offered you.

Chapter 6:

The Victim

HOW MANIPULATORS AFFECT YOUR BEHAVIOR

Have you ever had that impression in one of the relationships you have that something was not, quite right? Even with a casual gathering with someone you just met. Something just didn't feel quite right, and you are left feeling far more anxious, irritated, or confused than you were when you began. That could be a sign you have been in a manipulator's presence. The reason manipulators use the tactics they do is because they are often unable to simply ask what they need or be able to express their needs in a healthy, straightforward manner. Thus, they resort to this emotionally abusive tactic to try to manipulate other people around them and compel them to bend to their will.

Manipulation comes in various forms, and it can range from abusive to just being around a bossy personality anywhere. Some deceptive habits are much easier to spot than others, and if you believe you may be a psychological bully's target, these are the tell-tale signs for which you want to keep an eye out for:

YOU SENSE FEAR, DUTY, AND GUILT

Coercive conduct comprises three factors: anxiety, responsibility, and guilt. When someone manipulates you, you're mentally coerced to do something that you usually don't want to do. You could feel afraid to do so, compelled to do so, or guilty of not doing so.

I refer to two different manipulators: "the abuser" and "the victim." An abuser makes you feel afraid and will use violence, threats, and coercion to manipulate you. The victim instills a sense of guilt in their target. Usually, the victim acts hurt, although, the fact is they're the ones who created the problem. An individual approached by a manipulator who acts as the victim always attempts to support the manipulator to avoid feeling bad. Targets of this type of manipulation frequently feel responsible for assisting the victim to stop their suffering by doing everything they can.

STRINGS ARE CONNECTED

If you don't get a favor just because, then it's not "for fun and free."If strings are applied, then it is trickery.

One manipulator form is "Mr. Nice man". This person will be supportive and offer other people plenty of favors. It's complicated, but you don't know there is anything bad. But, on the other side, there is a rope connected for any positive deed — an obligation. If you don't fulfill the standards of the manipulator, you'll be forced to feel ungrateful. One of the most common forms of trickery is to exploit the rules and standards of reciprocity.

For example, a salesman could make it appear like you would purchase the product since he or she offered you a discount. A spouse in a partnership can buy you flowers and then ask for something in return. These techniques operate as it violates societal expectations. It's normal to return the favor but we often still feel it necessary to reciprocate and comply even if someone does one insincerely.

Manipulators frequently try out one of two strategies. The first one is the strategy of foot-in-the-door, in which somebody starts with a simple yet rational request — like, do you have a moment? — Which then contributes to a bigger request — like I want 10 dollars for a taxi. That's commonly used in street frauds.

The door-in-the-face method is the opposite — it includes somebody making a large request, having it rejected, and then asking a smaller favor.

E.g., anyone doing contract work can ask you for a large amount of money upfront, and afterward, ask for a lesser proportion after you've refused. This works since, according to me, the smaller appeal appears comparatively rational after the larger demand.

YOU INTERROGATE YOURSELF

Frequently, the term "gaslighting" is used to recognize manipulation that causes people to question themselves, their actuality, consciousness, or thoughts. A dishonest individual can distort what you're saying to make it about them, hijack the discussion or make you sound like you've done something bad when you're not entirely sure you've done it.

If you're being emotionally manipulated, you may experience a false sense of shame or defensiveness — like you utterly lost or had to do something wrong when, in fact, that's not the case.

"Blame the manipulators. They are not taking responsibility for this."

THE RELATIONSHIP MAKES YOU FEEL SCARED

Here's a general tip: if a relationship is built entirely out of a foundation of fear, then you know that it might not be a good one to be in. It's normal to feel intimidated or even somewhat fearful of certain people. Perhaps, you might be meeting someone you admire and idolize. To feel somewhat intimidated by that individual is okay to a certain degree. However, when you start building a close and intimate relationship with the person and the fear still doesn't go away, then that is a bad sign.

Manipulators understand fear very well, and they know how to use it against those who don't have good control over their phobias. For instance, say you've been planning something for a while and the person always comes up with last-minute changes that give them what they want, they are utilizing your fear of losing something. In this case, the time and emotional attachment were spent making and almost executing the plan. They will utilize the fear that you have of them into making you do things that would benefit them, even if it means compromising your well-being. This is why you should always be wary of relationship environments that reek of fear and intimidation.

YOU ARE MADE TO FEEL GUILTY ABOUT EVERYTHING YOU DO

Somehow, you are made to feel guilty about everything that you do. When you are in a manipulative relationship, nothing that you ever do will be right or correct.

Even when you have the best intentions and you are sure about your execution, there's still always something for you to feel bad about. Generally, a manipulative individual will avoid making you feel validated for your efforts or your actions. This is because they want you to feel like you need to work harder to be worthy of their attention and approval.

This is a tactic that is designed to bully a person into thinking that they're not doing enough so that they feel pressured to become better. It's a kind of negative reinforcement that is quite common in a lot of abusive relationships all over the world. It's the same way a boss would tell a worker that their work is mediocre to get that worker to keep on trying harder out of guilt or shame.

YOU OFTEN QUESTION YOUR OWN BELIEFS

Gaslighting is another common technique that is usually employed by manipulative individuals to distort an individual's view of reality. As a victim, you are made to doubt your own beliefs and perspectives on things so that you grow reliant and dependent on another person. Essentially, you are made to distrust your senses and instincts so that you will be forced to cling onto someone else to help you stay grounded and sane. Manipulative individuals are so good at distorting the facts and stretching the truth to the point that they make lies seem believable even when they're completely outrageous.

In essence, they are just thrusting their version of "reality" down your throat.

YOU ARE MADE TO FEEL LIKE THERE ARE ALWAYS STRINGS ATTACHED

Nothing you ever do in this kind of relationship will come without any strings attached. You just get the sense that if you will be on the receiving end of some nice treatment, it's never something that you can just take at face value. You notice that there's a pattern that's emerging here whenever this person does anything that adds value to your life. You always just come to expect that there will be some kind of ulterior motives behind it. You would find it very difficult to just take a compliment or be on the receiving end of a kind gesture. You somehow get the sense that that isn't the whole story.

YOUR INSECURITIES ARE ALWAYS THRUST INTO THE LIMELIGHT

One of the grandest ways in which a manipulative person would get you to become emotionally vulnerable would be to highlight your insecurities. Naturally, as a human being, you have your fair share of insecurities.

We all do,and the manipulative individual knows this better than anyone.

However, instead of being sensitive and empathetic toward these insecurities that you might have, they use it as ammo. They will capitalize on these insecurities to make you feel terrible about yourself, setting the brain into more reactive, survival mode.

In psychology, whenever an individual engages in self-hatred or self-loathing, they find a strong power figure to whom they can cling onto. The manipulative master knows this, and that's how they will want to present themselves in your life. They will make it seem like you need them to be there for you because of how incompetent you end up perceiving yourself to be. When you're with a manipulative person, you will constantly be bombarded with reminders of your vulnerabilities. Sparking insecurities or questioning people's identity to create "issues" people didn't know they had and then allaying these insecurities by offering the solution, is also a commonly used tactic in marketing.

YOU'RE STILL EXPECTED TO FORGET

If you don't go along with what they want, then they'll make you feel guilty. Even if you did have every right to say no. If you feel pressured continuously or compelled to do something you don't want to do, you are being manipulated. If you're afraid to say no, then you're manipulated. If you feel bothered to go along with the demands of someone else, you will be manipulated. Manipulators are experts in playing the victim card, and they will play it to make you feel as guilty as possible, as if you're doing something wrong because you've chosen to tell them no.

DOUBTING YOUR OWN JUDGMENT

You still find yourself questioning your own judgment every time you are around a particular person. Suddenly, after having a conversation with a manipulator, something you were so sure of a minute ago, fills you with doubt and makes you second guess your own decisions. Present them with an idea or an opinion, and they will somehow find a way to twist and turn it around, making you uncertain and uncomfortable. Spend enough time with them, and they will make you feel unworthy as if you were a complete failure, and nothing you could ever do is the right choice.

YOU'RE JUST BLAMING YOURSELF

Even though you've done nothing wrong, you're blaming yourself somehow. That one dishonest friend who always has an explanation for their bad conduct or poor judgment is not your friend,as they are always making you the scapegoat.

This one friend is a manipulator. It's your fault; you made me believe I should, if you thought it was a bad idea, I wouldn't have done it. A dishonest "friend's" trademark is when you're in the mix somewhere, and they are the ones who made you feel like you're wrong.

GLARING AND UNBELIEVABLE THINGS

They do glaring and unbelievable things, and then they try to convince you that what you saw wasn't true. What you saw couldn't be what you possibly think. It is because it doesn't look like you will do anything like that, and he would have to be a real idiot to do something like that to you. He wants to minimize his action and play ignorant like he has no idea what it is, and that you are tripping, because both of you are just friends. He also tries to make rude remarks in the name of humor.

WHY YOU ARE MANIPULATED

AN INABILITY TO SET BOUNDARIES OR TO SAY "NO."

Those who are easy to manipulate are generally so scared of confrontation that they are not willing to spark an argument by being resistant or by voicing their opinion. This specific trait is easy to exploit for obvious reasons—if they just cannot say no, you can burden them with favors and expectations, and anticipate no resistance in return.

HONESTY AND COMPASSION

Being honest makes you particularly manipulatable because your greatest weaknesses and loftiest aspirations are all apparent to those around you. Compassion, on the other hand, is the driving force for the first point in this list. Being overly compassionate opens you up to manipulation by those who are willing to play the victim, as master manipulators always are.

FEAR

This emotion comes in numerous structures. We, as human beings, tend to fear losing a relationship; we may fear the disapprobation of other people; we dread to make somebody discontent with our actions.

We additionally dread the dangers and outcomes of the manipulator's actions. Imagine a scenario in which they prevail at doing what they threaten.

GUILT

Today, we are clouded by the idea and responsibility that we should dependably prioritize the needs and wants of other people rather than our own. At times when people would talk about the right to fulfill their own needs and wants, manipulators frequently abuse us and endeavor to allow us to feel like we are accomplishing something immoral if we do not put their needs and wants in front of our own. Those individuals who are skilled at these manipulative tactics, would tend to define love as the act of fulfilling their needs and wants as part of your obligation. Hence, if we have an opinion that goes against their beliefs, we are manipulated into thinking that we are heartless; at this point, they will make us feel very regretful of our existence and would use guilt to manipulate us.

BEING TOO NICE

We appreciate being a provider, fulfilling individuals, and dealing with the needs of other people. We discover fulfillment. Moreover, our confidence would regularly originate from doing what we can for other people. In any case, at times when there is a lack of an unmistakable feeling of these and fair limitations, skilled manipulators can detect this in people who are easy targets of this phenomenon, and will use certain tactics to further their selfish gains.

UNCONDITIONAL LOVE

Those who are the absolute easiest to manipulate are those who unconditionally love the manipulator (parents, siblings, romantic partners, friends, etc.). The reason for this is that, regardless of the kind of treatment that they are forced to endure, they continue to love the manipulator. This love is an exploitable weakness.

BEING TRUSTING

People who are easy to manipulate believe anything you tell them, this is also known as "being too trusting." Some people are simply naïve, while others perhaps only see the best in the manipulator and refuse to acknowledge the uglier side—regardless of the reason, some people are easier to deceive than others.

BEING TOO POLITE OR RESPECTFUL

Manipulators actively seek out those who will not call them out in public, and who better to target than those who are too coy to say something when they are made to feel uncomfortable? Being overly polite also makes one more likely to agree to small favors which, as discussed earlier, makes one more likely to agree to larger and larger favors as time passes.

HOW TO AVOID BEING MANIPULATED

Similarly, it is just as important to know some tactics to avoid being manipulated yourself. The author of *Are You Too Nice? How to Gain Appreciation and Respect*, Ni Preston, developed eight techniques to avoid being manipulated.

The first technique he described is by far the easiest to abide by. It simply involves practicing the art of saying "no." If you feel uncomfortable with what is being asked of you, firmly say no. You do not necessarily need to be confrontational in doing this—a simple, "Sorry, I do not have time," will likely suffice.

The second technique is to set consequences. You need to handle a manipulator a little bit like you might handle a child: he or she needs to know the rules, and when he or she breaks these rules, there needs to be a "punishment." An example of how you could use this is by telling a person, "I am uncomfortable talking with you about that. If you continue to talk about it, I will report you to human resources." Manipulators do not want to get in trouble, so when trying to avoid being manipulated, make sure that you follow through on the rules and corresponding consequences that you have set.

The third technique is remembering that your time is your own, and you are allowed to take it. Manipulators will usually demand an answer to their requests immediately, in the hope of pressuring you into complying. You can circumnavigate this manipulative technique simply by saying, "I'll think about it." You don't have to follow a manipulator's timeline, and you are certainly not obligated to answer anything straight away.

The fourth technique involves asking manipulators probing questions when they make requests of you. Next time a manipulator asks you to do something for them, consider responding with, "Are you asking me, or telling me?" or "What do I get out of this?" or "Are you really expecting me to do that?" Chances are, you will catch the manipulator off-guard and perhaps even get them to withdraw the request completely (at the very least, it will force them to pause for a second and consider whether what they are doing is right).

The fifth technique is to avoid letting the manipulator make you feel guilty. You are not obligated to do anyone any favors, and thus, you have nothing to feel guilty about. Manipulators make their targets feel guilty in the hope that they will eventually feel so bad about themselves that they will give in to the manipulator's will.

The sixth technique is to keep your distance. If you know that somebody is manipulating you (or trying to), do not give them any opportunities to do so by spending time with them. It is honestly good advice just to give a manipulator a wide berth and to avoid getting pulled into their games altogether.

The seventh technique is to know your rights. Manipulators will go out of their way to violate them. Remind yourself regularly that you have the right to be treated with respect, to set your own priorities, to have a differing opinion, and to express your feelings.

The eighth, and final, the technique is to confront the manipulator. Publicly. A manipulator will generally avoid the public eye, and by calling them out, you are likely to put them off trying to manipulate you ever again.

DEALING WITH A TOXIC PERSON

Other indications to keep a watch out are if the individual is constantly condescending, compulsively in desire, or unwilling to take accountability or say sorry for one's behavior.

It may be anyone who regularly takes narcotics or alcohol, lies or wants you to lie about them, regulates or demeans what you've been doing. A toxic man's life is always personally, emotionally, financially, physically, or interpersonally out of balance.

SETTING BOUNDARIES TO ELIMINATE MANIPULATORS

"If you feel unnoticed or misunderstood and feel manipulated or compelled to do stuff that is not even 'you,' then you may be affected by a negative human." Toxic individuals can make you question yourself or unconsciously do something that you wouldn't normally do—you might feel a need to be fit in or cool or get approval. Every situation is different, but by influencing people to do something, toxic individuals may have a detrimental effect on others.

They try to generate turmoil by negative behaviors: to use, to lie, to steal, to control, to criticize, to bully, to manipulate, to create conflict, and so on.

EFFECT OF TOXIC PEOPLE ON YOUR LIFE

Toxic individuals can impact all aspects of people's lives, and we are always oblivious to that. We feel sympathy for them. The myths they inflict on us are accepted and rationalized. And this, in exchange, changes how we look about our values and ourselves. Toxic individuals are happy to drive happiness down from the stuff we previously enjoyed, such as jobs, relationships, interests, and even our self-love.

DEALING WITH MANIPULATORS WHO ARE A PERMANENT PART OF YOUR LIFE

If a manipulator had been in your life for a while, you might have already ceded some level of control over your life to him by now, so you have to start by regaining that control. First, you have to create and enforce boundaries in your life.

To set and enforce boundaries, you have to assess different areas of your life and set firm limits in all of those areas. You have to draw a line, and you have to make it clear to the manipulator that he or she is not allowed to cross that boundary. For example, you can set aside some "me time" and tell everyone that they are not allowed to bother you during that time.

Setting boundaries will help you reestablish the priorities in your life. If you have been a victim of manipulation, chances are the manipulator has spent months or even years establishing control over your life, so that by the point you know what's going on, he may have replaced your priorities with his own. You may find that you are using all your free time to do things he likes, and your interests have taken a back seat to his.

When you find yourself in such a situation, bouncing back can be hard, but it's going to require a lot of willpower and commitment on your part. Take control of your own life. Create a list of all your values and reexamine all of them. Look at your belief system, and question everything that you believe about yourself; did you always hold those beliefs, or did you acquire them over time as you got closer to the manipulative person?

If you notice that your time is spent doing things that don't interest you, your belief system has been infiltrated by ideas that aren't originally yours, and that your long term values no longer seem to be the driving force behind your life, you need to create new boundaries and rules for yourself to keep the manipulative person from controlling you.

You need to disconnect from manipulative people, especially the ones whose machinations have caused you (or could potentially cause you) serious psychological or physical harm. One mistake most victims make is that they assume that they can change the manipulator. They convince themselves that if they spend enough time with the manipulator, he will fall in love with them, and he will be open to treating them better. However, in the end, the opposite happens. Instead of the victim changing the manipulator as she may have hoped, it's the manipulator that changes her, and not for the better. She starts accepting the emotional abuse, and little by little, she makes concessions about her values and principles, until, in the end, she is a completely different person. She becomes more subservient, and she starts making excuses for the manipulator.

So, once you notice that someone is manipulating you, the best choice you have is to disconnect from them. If a clean break is possible, you should go for it. However, in situations where it's a lot more complicated (for example, where you have children together) a clean break might not be possible. Even then, spending some time away from the manipulator can help you re-enter yourself so that you can remember what your real values and priorities used to be.

Chapter 7:

What Is Manipulation? Why Manipulation Is Wrong & Why People Manipulate

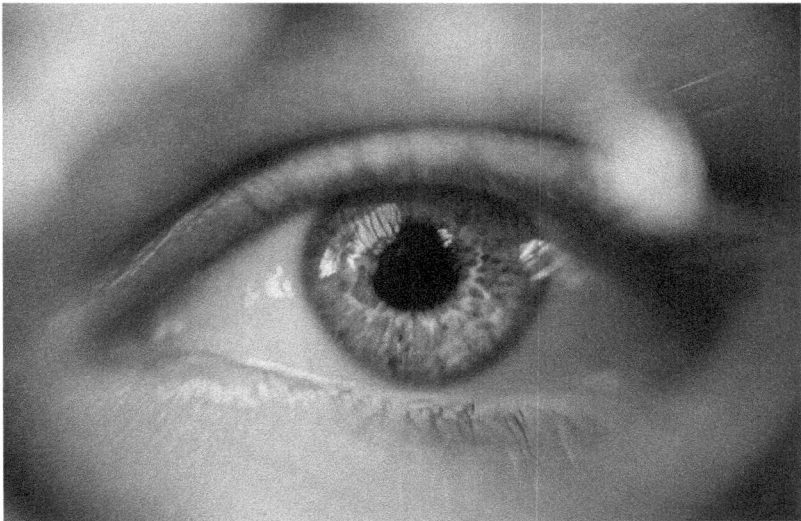

WHAT IS MANIPULATION

Manipulation is - in psychology - a method deliberately implemented to control or influence the thinking, choices, actions of an individual, via a relationship of power or influence. The methods used to distort or orient the perception of the interlocutor's reality by using, in particular, a relationship of seduction, suggestion, persuasion, involuntary or consented submission.

Manipulation is part of the daily lives of civilizations.In the modern West, power systems, conflicts of interest, power struggles are omnipresent: it develops from self-awareness, language, and the hierarchy of society which produce a large number of interactions from which everyone wants to benefit from. It is a learned skill that forms part of the culture, and which everyone knows and uses in their personal or professional life, in a positive or negative, conscious, or unconscious way. In such a civilization, any communication (body language or oral language) can, thus, be a form of influence or manipulation.

A manipulative person uses indirect means to make a person change their actions or thoughts. Some of the indirect tactics include persuasion and brainwashing. In persuasion, a person does not force you to do something, but they try to convince you to do it. A good example of persuasion in marketing. Although an advertisement is aimed directly at convincing you to purchase a certain item, you are not in any way forced to purchase it. The choice to buy it or not is in your hands. The only aspect that an advertiser works on is to ensure that you see the beauty of the item. The advertiser will only tell you about the good aspects of the item you are trying to buy without mentioning the negatives. Even those who choose to mention the negatives, also try to show them as slightly positive aspects. This is an indirect way of luring someone into making a purchase.

Manipulation is a way of socially influencing you into doing something you did not necessarily want to do. However, this does not mean that social influence in and on itself is something bad. Social influence can be used for a good cause. You can influence someone to stop taking drugs or change some unhealthy habits. When you persuade a person to do such actions, it cannot be termed as manipulation. Social influence only becomes a manipulative habit if it is aimed at benefiting the influencer. If you can persuade someone into taking another job just to benefit from their salary, you are a manipulator. Most manipulative individuals do not deem their actions harmful in any way. When a person is using manipulation tactics, they aim to benefit without directly being seen as a bad person. In most cases, a manipulative person will lure you into doing something bad and end up blaming you for it. In simple terms, a manipulative individual uses other people as puppets. You are just a tool that the manipulator uses to achieve a certain goal. A manipulative person can use you to steal money and end up putting all the blame on you.

There is a whole range of methods ranging from cunning, an action that can be legitimate, to the most degrading forms of psychic manipulation, including all kinds of lies. Manipulation as a scientific concept is mainly studied in social psychology and philosophy.

Mental manipulation induces a power relationship that results in the psychic control of a person. More precisely, it is "the modification of an individual's mental state by another to make him do something." This can be summed up in "fabricated consent."

In social psychology, the term "conditioning," is a word that appeared in the 14th century and developed following Pavlov's work. "Since then, and by extension, conditioning represents the mental or psychic conditions necessary for the performance of a behavior."

We distinguish the influence of manipulation, even if they use the same tools and psychological springs. If they are just as difficult to detect: the impact implies a transparent motivation while the manipulation includes deception without any benefit. In psychology, manipulation is defined as a secret action of a person or group of persons. The whole art of manipulation consists in depriving the manipulated of his freedom without realizing it, and that he is persuaded to be free.

The propaganda or publicity-seeking to mobilize the behavior of short-term masses, sometimes is achieved using irrational means. According to its use as a weapon of war, it is used as propaganda to manipulate public opinion. Disinformation is "probably one of the most difficult manipulations to detect and identify," and it is one of the main weak points of the information society.

The packaging is in the long-term by forming habits and playing on emotions. The indoctrination educates, also for a long time, addressing the beliefs and intelligence.

THE MANIPULATION ETHICS — COULD MANIPULATION BE GOOD AND BAD?

At the mention of the word 'manipulation,' negative connotations associated with this term is what immediately springs to mind. Manipulation means taking advantage of someone else by unscrupulous and underhanded tactics. Manipulation means theft and lying outright. Manipulation is unethical. Through the years, the word has had a poor reputation, and even the phrases used to characterize deception in play, depict an image that is quite nasty or negative. "She's got him wrapped around her little finger," "I told my boss exactly what he wanted to hear," "He's got a reputation for being a heartbreaker," "I spoke to my buddy about doing what I wanted." These traditional manipulative scenarios don't make a positive difference to the situation for the parties involved in the transaction. It makes the manipulator greedy, self-serving, deceitful, and unconcerned about manipulating someone else for their gain, and it makes the one being manipulated seem stupid, ignorant, and maybe even weak to "allow" himself to be so easily fooled.

85

Manipulation has always been seen as a cruel, smart, yet cunning act and always where one person ends up being manipulated. Manipulation is seen even more negatively when it is clear that the conniving person has a heartless presence, disregarding the other's feelings and placing their own selfish needs above all others. Even worse than the manipulator, he exploited the other by pretending to be his friend and then using trustfully shared information against them. There is one fact that remains in our personal or professional lives. No-one wants to learn that they were abused. Nobody. Such uncertainty associated with it is hard andit is almost painful to imagine that there is a possibility that it might be used to exploit a positive, or even that it could bring about change for the better. Manipulation isn't all evil; however, shocking it might sound. There is manipulation all around us, and often you don't have to look very far to find evidence of it. Take, for example, marketers and advertisers, with their constant messages telling us to buy this, buy that, stop doing this, and stop doing that. They all try to influence our decisions one way or the other. However, what kinds of manipulation are trying to make us change for the better?

Ads that advise us to stop smoking and eat better are trying to exploit our choices, but they're trying to do so, in this case, to promote positive change. Quitting smoking is in your own best interestsand it feeds well. Would this not make it a constructive way of manipulation, if it is for your good? Governments around the world are exploiting their people. Religion does, likewise. Yet, sometimes we choose to ignore it because it comes, so to speak, from a more "authoritative" source. Businesses are actively exploiting their customers by producing goods to raise their sales figures and then telling consumers, "without them, they cannot survive."

Whether it's utilized for "good" or "bad," manipulation is still manipulation, at the end of the day. Does any of us have any right to dictate the decisions or actions of another, even if we believe this is to their advantage? What makes the thought of manipulation so upsetting is maybe the fact that we don't like someone elsetrying to decide what we can door forcing us to do anything we wouldn't be inclined to do ourselves otherwise. Working managers try to manipulate their staff all the time, even if the good leaders do it to try and keep their staff motivated or performing their best. Active managers have mastered the art of motivational reinforcement skillfully and have turned it into an important method used to influence the success of their workers, driving them to achieve their objectives. That distinctive detail is the defining difference between what is classified as manipulation and what is called persuasion. Persuasion is a form of manipulation, but what distinguishes it from the negative image of manipulation lies in three things:

Aim.

Honesty.

What gain or positive effect the person you're trying to convince would have.

WHY ARE WE VULNERABLE TO MANIPULATION?

It is not enough to know the definition of manipulation; it is still necessary to discover the reasons for our vulnerability to manipulation. Of course, they are multiple and different from one person to another. In general, a first large group of explanations stems from motivation and its two great strengths: the avoidance of suffering and the pursuit of pleasure.

So, a manipulative person can motivate you to do whatever they want because they strike a chord with you and cause discomfort or an emotion that you don't want to feel. No one likes to suffer and feel guilt, fear, insecurity, helplessness, doubt, etc. So, in this case, you are being manipulated because you want to avoid suffering.

When your self-image is somewhat flawed; in other words, when you are unsure of yourself, of what you are, of what you want, manipulation can more easily cause you to doubt or guilt. For example, someone is sulking because you said or did something. To avoid the guilt, you say that you didn't mean it rather than endure this sulking (which is a form of passive aggression). Example number 3 above is a good illustration of this.

Besides, manipulation tactics can also touch one of your fears, such as that of being judged. No one likes to be criticized for being selfish, incompetent, ungrateful, or inhuman. It can also be the fear of hurting, not being loved, losing an advantage, losing affection, respect, a material advantage, or even your job.

The manipulative person may control your behavior by giving you the hope of some sort of gain. It will make you hope for an emotional advantage, attention, recognition, status, even love, or a material advantage such as career advancement, reaching your goals more efficiently, obtaining results, and tangible rewards.

Here you are in the other great force of motivation: the search for pleasure.

Of course, both types of motivation can coexist in each of us, depending on the context. However, you probably have one strategy that takes precedent over the other, some sort of mental program that influences your actions, no matter what decisions you have to make. Some are more motivated by the stick or by avoidance; for others, it is the prospect of gain that motivates them to act. Recognizing this underlying tendency in you may help you understand how you come to be manipulated.

WHY DO PEOPLE USE MANIPULATION?

TO GAIN WEALTH

People use manipulation to fulfill their desires in life. If you want money, you may use any means possible to get a good job. This is a very big motivation for most people across cultures. All over the world, people use manipulation just to get wealth. Since money is a valuable asset in life, it can give you access to most of your desires and most people will do anything just to earn money. Such motivation will make most people use manipulation.

TO MAINTAIN THEIR INTEGRITY

Many people use manipulation just to keep their names clean. If a person has evil intentions but does not want the world to see them, they will use manipulation. Narcissists use manipulation and blackmail to hide their weaknesses. A narcissistic person may even ruin your name in public or lower your self-esteem just to avoid showing the world that they are weak. Most people who are striving to maintain social authenticity may go to extreme limits in their drive to maintain social standings.

TO GAIN INFLUENCE

The other reason why people use manipulation is to gain influence. Social influence gives people power. Most people enjoy it when they have power and control over others. We have talked about the example of political leaders and how they use manipulative tactics just to gain control over the masses. Politicians will do anything possible as long as they gain control. It is normal for people to employ such tactics in their search for power and influence. A person who wants power and influence will approach you with lies and trickery just to gain power over you.

TO DOMINATE RELATIONSHIPS

Most people feel safe when they are the dominating voice in a relationship. It is normal for human beings to want to have control over a relationship. This desire to control a relationship may make a person want to manipulate others. Manipulation will help those individuals control their relationship partner and, thus, gain control of any related assets. The main reason behind that desire to have control is the fear of the unknown. If a person that is afraid of uncertainty is in a relationship and does not have clear knowledge of the future, they may use underhand methods to control the relationship.

SELF-SATISFACTION

In some instances, people who use manipulation are just looking for a way to satisfy their ego. Many individuals suffer low self-esteem and only find satisfaction in controlling others. You may be in a manipulative relationship trying to figure out what you did that was wrong. In some cases, you may do everything right, but still become a victim of manipulation. People practice manipulation just to feel satisfied and happy. Such people have deeply rooted emotional and psychological issues that need to be addressed by an expert.

WHAT ARE PEOPLE'S REASONS FOR MANIPULATING OTHERS?

Misery likes company: They do it because they gain satisfaction on an emotional level, from seeing the frustrated or negative responses of others. Certain people are so unhappy with their lives and themselves that they try to bring others down by creating problems for them.

It makes them feel powerful: Someone who is insecure and feels powerless will often try to exert power in other areas to make up for it. Getting others to do what they want gives them temporary satisfaction.

A lack of importance: Another reason why people negatively manipulate others is that they don't think that they are important. They believe that if they simply request what they wish for, they won't get it because they don't matter enough. So instead, they try to make us feel ashamed or guilty as a consequence for not doing what they want, as a preemptive measure from disappointment.

They are "too good" for some things: Other negative manipulators simply think that they are too good for certain tasks. They might see other people as below them, and therefore, expect those people to do the tasks that they don't want to do. This could be due to laziness, or simply an inflated sense of self.

Not knowing how to get things done: Some negative manipulators don't think that they are capable of gaining what they want, and instead operate under the assumption that they must convince and pressure others to do their bidding for them.

Selfishly "helping" others: Other negative manipulators convince themselves that what they are doing will help people. This is a common idea embraced by people who think that they know better than others what is best for everyone. Due to their beliefs that they have a higher intelligence or ability, they feel satisfied doing this and convince themselves that the people being manipulated are better off for it. The majority of negative manipulators are not bad people; they are simply misguided, inconsiderate, insensitive, selfish, and often, weak and insecure. Some of them believe that the people they are manipulating are not as valuable as themselves and that their desires and needs are not as important. This mistaken belief is what allows them to continue to act the way they do without considering the feelings of other people.

DIFFERENT TYPES OF NEGATIVE MANIPULATION

Turning your emotions against you: Techniques for manipulation vary widely, but usually, negative manipulators will attempt to get the feelings of others to work against them. They will try to do that by doing or saying things that are intended to stir up fear, anger, shame, guilt, or any other uncomfortable feeling. For example, they might insinuate that if we don't follow through on their suggestions or orders, something horrible will result.

Threats of future unpleasantness: They might also try to describe to you all the different types of unpleasant situations that could arise if you don't do what they want. They might imply or even overtly insist that something is our fault, responsibility, or duty, using ethics and morality to pressure us to come around to their ideas or demands. Some people will even throw every trick at us, warning us of the consequences of disappointing or letting them down.

Common phrases used: They may imply to us that we will be so happy if we do what they want us to do, or that we will make them very happy, and that they will love us so much. They may also use phrases like "You need to…" or "You must…" or "You should…" as a way to subtly pressure you into following through on what they are asking of you. They will say those phrases and others which insinuate great consequences if you don't follow the obligation they are giving to you.

What does each of the above methods and techniques share with each other? The person doing the negative manipulation doesn't offer anything of value in return for fulfilling their wishes. Instead, the victim gets exploited by a created power imbalance.

EXAMPLES OF MANIPULATION

There are many real-life examples of manipulation happening right next to you in your daily life. If you are keen enough, you may be able to notice how certain people use manipulation and blackmail to have things their way in life. It is common to spot such cases in the workplace. In family situations, manipulation comes in place when there is something valuable at stake. For instance, if a wealthy person dies without leaving a clear will, there will be many people fighting to take control of the properties of the deceased.

A real-life example of manipulation would be the case of Jonestown (Guyana). The story of Jonestown is one of the most documented cases of manipulation and brainwashing. The mastermind behind the story being Jim Jones, who was a religious/cult leader.

Jim Jones rose to fame in Northwest Guyana during the early 70s. His rise to fame was associated with supernatural affairs. Like all manipulative individuals, Jones managed to gather a small group of brainwashed individuals around himself.

One of the key characteristics of manipulative individuals is isolation, as we have already said. However, manipulators who wish to gain public influence and control large crowds of people, do not just use isolation. Most public manipulators use the inner circle approach. An inner circle is made up of people who subscribe to the ideologies of the manipulator. The ideologies are often deemed as right, and they are not seen to have anything wrong. This is an approach that most cultic sects take. When a person is introduced in the inner circle, they make them feel special, but at the same time, they are required to fulfill certain conditions. In most cases, you will find that members of the inner circle are required to pledge allegiance to the leader of the sect.

Like all sects, Jim Jones started creating a small circle of people who would later work as recruiters. The entire village of Jonestown started subscribing to the ideologies and teachings of Jones. After some time, many people subscribed to his teachings. The social pressure associated with the people joining the sect attracted even more people. The more people gathered to the sect, the more manipulative the man became. In the mid-1970s, Jim Jones pronounced himself as being a god who had come to rescue the people from their predicaments. Given that the case happened at a time when people were suffering from poor economic status, the leader took advantage of the situation. The poor villagers were drawn to him hoping that he was going to make their lives better. They gave their attention to him and allowed him to take control of all their lives.

Just like all manipulative leaders, Jim Jones did not care about the welfare of the people. He did not provide whatever he promised. Instead, he used his popularity to amass wealth from the victims. He lured the victims into giving him sexual favors and managed to control the whole village.

The story of Jim Jones climaxed with the massacre of over 900 people who followed the sect leader. The town was named after this merciless sect leader who did not bother to think about the welfare of the people. As a manipulative person, he did not mind killing 900 people just to get whatever he wanted. Although the story of Jonestown is an extreme case that looks at a person who showed sociopathic tendencies, it reveals the true character of a manipulative person. Most manipulators do not care about how you feel or what you think. They aim to gain and move on with life.

Chapter 8:

Manipulation Tactics

BEST MANIPULATION TECHNIQUES

DISTRACTION STRATEGY

This is one of the most common manipulation techniques used by governments, political parties, world leaders, politicians, and other public personalities to divert the public attention from the vital problems by introducing continuous distractions and trivial/unimportant information.

This way, the public attention remains fixated on insignificant issues, while the true political and social issues are hidden under the carpet. It gives the public the illusion of being busy with something, though that something is of little consequence in their life. They don't have the time to think about the negative impact of important issues in their lives and the inability of their leaders to resolve these issues.

CREATE PROBLEMS THAT DON'T EXIST AND OFFER SOLUTIONS

This is another classic social manipulation strategy that is widely used throughout the world. It consists of creating an imaginary or foreseen issue to stimulate a specific reaction among victims of manipulation or the public. Then, the manipulator carefully introduces a solution to become the ultimate messiah.

For example, allowing urban violence to build and thrive initially or supporting terrorist camps. This can be followed by making people aware of how their security is the government's prime concern and how leaders will go all out to intensify security measures to ensure public safety.

You introduce a problem and then offer a solution without letting the victims realize that you were directly responsible for creating the problems. This way, you become the solution provider, who can get people to act in a desired manner.

THE PAINFUL REALITY

Let us consider a scenario to understand this strategy clearly.

Your boss urges everyone at the workplace to put in additional hours of work or to work during weekends. He or she may lead you to believe that you all stand to lose your jobs and the market is tight, which means that you have to step up and go the extra mile to survive. They will inform you about how other companies who

97

weren't able to bag big projects couldn't sustain operation costs and eventually closed down.

The managers will convince you how a few sacrifices from your side can go a long way in saving the company's fortunes. Do you see what they are doing there? They are projecting their decision as painful yet necessary. They'll tell how they don't want you to stay late at work, but there's no other option if you want to keep your job or for the company to stay afloat. A majority will resign to the idea of working late.

TO PROJECT VICTIMS AS IGNORANT OR STUPID

The easiest way to get people to do what you want them to do publicly, professionally, or socially is to make them feel how ignorant or stupid they are or how they don't understand something. For instance, if you are looking to introduce new technology that will save labor costs and increase profits, you may have a bunch of people rebelling against it for fear of losing their jobs.

By using the ignorant manipulation tactic, you inform people about how they cannot comprehend technology which is designed to make things easier. You are playing on their lack of awareness or uncertainty about a thing. You are telling them that they aren't in a position to give their view or opinion about it because they do not have the right knowledge or understanding of these systems.

Again, you are replacing revolt with guilt, by making the victims feel like they are responsible for their unfortunate situation or their lack of intelligence/capabilities.

Thus, instead of rebelling, workers blame or devalue themselves, inhibiting further action.

DROWN THEM WITH FACTS, INFORMATION, AND STATISTICS

Emotional manipulation doesn't work on everyone, especially in social and professional settings. Here, people are more inclined to follow the logic and rational arguments. Drown these folks in information by quoting research, facts, figures, statistics, and more.

Have numbers ready on your fingertips for any objections and clarifications. Overwhelm people with statistics, logical arguments, and research. Be armed with the vital information to "intellectually bully" people. Present yourself as the ultimate authority or the source of knowledge in a particular field. Cleverly present research that supports your stand or point of view. Take advantage of established expertise to the fullest.

One of the best ways to manipulate people with logic is to present research, statistics, and figures in a compelling and imposing manner. Focus on areas where you believe they may not have sound knowledge and question them about it. This establishes their weakness in their own eyes. They will realize that they have little or no information about this area and that you are more experienced or knowledgeable than them.

This will automatically increase your chances of getting them to do what you want. This technique works well during business negotiations, sales, social debates, and other social or public settings.

You gain a smart subconscious edge over the other person, which makes them more defenseless and open to listening to you. It creates a sort of intellectual superiority, which makes them feel inadequate and compels them to comply with your demands.

THE VICTIM TALKS FIRST

When you are getting another party to agree to your negotiation terms or buy from you, allow them to talk first. This allows you as a persuader, influencer, or manipulator to establish their baseline. What are their strengths and weaknesses? What are their thoughts, emotions, fears, and behavior patterns? Are they more hesitant or self-confident? Do they appear extroverted/open or introverted/closed? Are they approaching the deal or sales with an element of hesitation? Are they overwhelmed by your presence? What does their body language reveal about them?

Allowing them to communicate first, helps you set a baseline for both their strengths and weaknesses, which can be utilized to get them to act in the desired direction. You can also prepare a list of questions that you can ask them to establish a baseline. The idea is to get them thinking in the direction of acting in your favor. For instance, if you are planning to sell insurance, you ask them a list of questions that help you establish their fears and, therefore, allow you to play on these fears for getting them to sign up quickly.

TWEAK THE ENVIRONMENT TO GAIN ADVANTAGE

You can use the right environment at the right time to ask for someone to do something for you. Debunk the theory that there is a place and time for everything and make the environment work in your favor. For instance, if you are partying with a boss or coworker on a Friday night, instead of waiting until Monday morning to ask them for a favor, use the relaxed setting of a pub or bar. They'll be less guarded, more chilled out and relaxed, and in a more positive mood. Your chances of getting them to agree to the favor may be higher in a more relaxed setting, where they don't expect you to ask for such a favor. Change the setting of where you'd normally ask something like this to increase your chances of getting people to agree.

CRITICISM

This is whereby the manipulator uses tactics such as belittling, dismissing, and ridiculing you. This keeps someone off-balance. Negative criticism is directed at a partner that makes them feel unworthy. The act of criticizing enables them to gain control over you. The manipulator creates a narrative that there is always something wrong with you and you are not good enough. This kind of narrative makes you doubt yourself, often of what you feel and know. It reaches a point where you do not trust yourself.

USING FLATTERY, KINDNESS, AND CHARM

The use of kindness, charm, and flattery is often more damaging than you realize. The generous deployment of these techniques is known as a passive-aggressive type of behavior. The manipulator uses tactics such as gifting someone items, massaging their egos with flattery, and lots of compliments. One is left to question the real reason behind the compliments, expensive gifts, and paying lots of attention to the victim. These are acts done with ulterior motives, especially when they realize you are about to catch up on the manipulative state. Bribery is also another technique of manipulating someone. It yields results when implemented. Bribery is a better technique than blackmailing an individual. You can even entice a friend with a better offer. The reward doesn't have to be of monetary value. It can be something that you would have done anyway or had already done prior. Perhaps, in the process of asking for help in your studies from a colleague, you can decide to offer her a lunch treat after studying in exchange.

LYING

Lying is normally used by con artists. Manipulators lie about everything they see, hear, or know. They create lies that are so complex that they tend to wrap people up in ways that they cannot differentiate between reality and fake life. These lies can only be disputed by checking for inconsistency in the stories. When the deal is too good, think twice before accepting an offer. Abusers use this manipulation technique as they do not have fears about it. Lying can be caught if the victim decides to do a background check on the sources of information.

HAVING THE HOME COURT ADVANTAGE

The process of manipulating an individual all depends on the level of control one has over the other. A manipulator will insist on meeting and having your interactions in an area he is comfortable with.

This technique is used to gain an edge of control over someone by taking them out of their element. The places where you normally spend time, are usually his spots and not yours. These places include his office, house, vehicle, and hanging out joints. Such areas make the manipulator exercise his dominance. People are easy to control when he is uneasy with the environment.

This technique can be done away with when the victim makes it clear that meeting places should be where they are both comfortable. Restaurantsand events to attend should be chosen by both of you. This leads to a partnership, breeding a healthy relationship in the process.

CARESSING THE EGO

Caressing the ego is most common in personal relationships. The manipulator caresses the ego of the victim by feeding her lies. The ego grows with time and in the end, the manipulator has you on his leash.

This technique can be avoided if the victim of the act possesses humility.

MAKING UNUSUAL REQUEST BEFORE YOUR REAL REQUEST

This kind of manipulation technique is a slight "mind game" oriented. The tactic involves asking an unusual request, mostly of a higher degree. This throws the person off balance, as he wasn't expecting such a request. The manipulator knew how that person was likely to respond if he would have asked for the usual request such as money, favor, shoes. The victim was more likely to respond "no" because people's minds have been conditioned to avoid these tasks.

For instance, a salesperson knows approaching someone on the street and asking him to buy the items being sold would likely lead to no sale. The salesman would first ask the potential client to do something such as help him with directions. This will build a "relationship" with the person and makes them less likely to turn you down in your presentation.

VOICE RAISING AND IRATE OUTBURSTS

Manipulators raise their voices during arguments to intimidate someone. They believe this process of raising the voice aggressively or loudly can enable them to achieve what they wanted. In a relationship, passion can come out in different forms such as tenderness, cute smiles you give one another, laughter, and the desire to share warmth in the arms of another. Passion, however, should not be mistaken by angry unpredictable outbursts during disagreements. In marriages or couples where they tend to disagree with one another,it is not uncommon. There are various ways of handling conflict, such as, having healthy communication with your partner andnot screaming or having temper tantrums. The aggressive voice is sometimes accompanied by strong body language.

The manipulator can also start to pick quarrels about non-issues. When this starts to occur, it's a display telling you there are items that need to be ironed out. There are forces at play. In a relationship, someone who's picking random quarrels is either cheating on the partner or looking to end the relationship.

INSPIRING FEAR OVER A PARTNER THEN RELIEF

This technique of manipulation tends to have a high rate of success over its victims. It normally involves making someone fear that the worst will happen by creating stories or giving out the wrong information. If the story does not happen, that person is likely to be relieved, and then he would be happy enough to grant you whatever you want. It's all about playing mind games with the victim.

DOING A FAVOR

When offered something, the humans feel indebted and generally try, as quickly as possible, to render a service in return to feel relieved, and thus, to let go of this feeling of obligation which they feel. This is mainly why many brands give free samples out of their products!

Consciously or not, in the human mind, incurring a debt brings about the fact of having to repay it. It is a rule which is the cement of the social bond, even in primitive human societies. However, the violation of the law of reciprocity is wrongly perceived, which makes it successful. This is why doing a service builds a bond of trust with the person and makes them more easily manipulated afterward. Angry, for owing someone something.

Another aspect of the rule of reciprocity: there is another principle, that of reciprocal concession. When an individual formulates a request that we refuse at first and reformulates his request, he makes a concession, and we, therefore, tend to respond with a reciprocal admission. To manipulate someone, ask for something rather than

104

giving something. For example, ask for a small favor rather than rendering one. Or, ask for something you don't really want and then rephrase your request by pretending to make a concession.

USE THE PERSON'S FIRST NAME

The human brain needs to be able to name actions, things, and people. A name on a face and presto, it's no longer unknown. It is no longer "the mass." A first name, just like a word, helps make things concrete.

Besides, the first name is often the first word known and remembered by a baby. Therefore, this creates a unique connection between the baby's first name and himself—a kind of anchor. Suddenly, people who use their first name to address someone (even if they hardly know him), immediately seem more sympathetic and familiar. These are the two criteria that promote manipulation.

Have you ever heard someone say your first name without speaking to you? Yet inevitably, you turned around or at least felt concerned at that point. It was stronger than you! This is proof that there is a strong emotional anchor between your first name and you. So, the next time a stranger asks for your first name and uses it to formulate his requests, you'll know he's trying to manipulate you!

FLATTERY

Contrary to popular belief, flattery is a manipulation technique that works. However, you need to think a minimum of what you say.

If you respect this condition, then even if the person knows that you are petting them, they will be sensitive. However, be careful, this technique does not work if the person you are trying to manipulate does not think you are sincere.

Flattery is a technique of manipulation that belongs to the family of displays of love. We create a pseudo-spirit of family and belonging through embracing emotional displays, affection, and flattery. It is very beneficial because the individual immediately feels taken in by a new family.

GIVE A REASON

Our brain is hardwired to accept more of a request when it comes with a reason. Even if it's a shitty reason, "Can I go ahead of you in the queue because I have to go make photocopies afterward?"

Know that to manipulate people; you can choose to give a justification. Even if your argument is flawed, the person will be tempted to say "yes" to you. More, in any case, than if you don't bother to argue.

STEP IN THE DOOR

The foot in the door is a well-known manipulation technique. Asking someone for a small favor is a great way to build a persuasive "dynamic." Then you present your "real" request to him.

This technique is a logical continuation of that which consisted in being rendered a small service. Except that here, instead of playing on reciprocity, we are playing on commitment and consistency.

If the person answered yes to your first request or did you a little favor, you could ask for something more substantial.

The person is expected to say yes because they want to justify the fact that they have already helped you and because you have built a pseudo-relationship of trust.

THE DOOR IN THE NOSE

The trick relies on the power of human guilt. It is the reverse of the foot in the door. Here you will ask for something huge or ridiculous to get a no.

When the NO answer finally comes to you, you present a second request, which is more reasonable (but genuine from the start, of course).

By the way, if by some mystery the person accedes to your first "huge" request, so much the better! But more often than not, she will accept the second instead.

THE RED SCARF

The red scarf technique involves reluctantly pretending to refuse something to have a better chance of getting a reward (which you wanted from the start).

Example to better understand is a divorce where we would insist on having the dog. At the last moment, we would reluctantly pretend to give it up in compensation for something else like a trinket (which we wanted from the start). The other party will leave it to us, thinking they've won.

THE GUILT

Guilt is a technique that can be used to manipulate someone. But be aware that, depending on who you come across, it can also irritate them and have the opposite effect.

To make someone feel guilty is to say to them, "I thought I could count on you," and that sort of thing.

Chapter 9:

How to Help Someone Being Controlled

Y ou will encounter manipulative people in your life – there is no question about it. So, you must learn how to deal with them. There are two kinds of manipulators that you will deal with; those you can avoid (strangers, casual acquaintances, etc.) and those who are a permanent fixture in your life (family members, close friends, colleagues, etc.).

When it comes to strangers and casual accountancies, once you notice that they are manipulative, you can keep your interactions with them at a minimum. However, if it's someone close to you, dealing with them will be a lot more complicated, and it requires a lot of effort and commitment on your part.

When you encounter a manipulative person, the most important thing you can do is to keep your emotions in check and try to be as logical as possible. So, first, you need to stay calm. Manipulators know that they are more likely to get what they want when you react emotionally, so they'll do whatever they can to get a rise out of you or to emotionally destabilize you in one way or another.

So, the best thing you can do at that moment is to take a breath, calm yourself, and try to think clearly. For example, when a manipulator asks you to do something, he will keep pushing you because he wants you to say "Yes" right away. He wants you to make an instant emotional decision because he knows that if you take your time, think things over, weigh the pros and cons before making a decision; you are more likely to choose an option that isn't in your own best interest. From this point on, you should be wary of any person who tries to force you to decide the heat of the moment.

Often, manipulators will try to create a sense of urgency (a salesman may try to tell you that he is running out of stock, or your partner might give you an ultimatum). Approach every interaction with the understanding that decision making (no matter how small it may seem) is an executive function and not an emotional one, so anyone who wants you to make an emotional decision is technically a manipulator.

To help people avoid making emotional decisions in the heat of the moment, some psychologists recommend the use of grounding techniques to deal with strong emotions. For example, if you feel stressed or anxious, you can ground yourself by focusing all of your attention on what you are feeling in your body at the moment (if for instance, your heart is racing, focus your mind on your racing heart;

this will keep your mind from racing all over the place, and it will help calm you down).

Once you have your emotions in check, the next thing you need to do is learn to say a firm "no." Many of us find it difficult to turn people down outright. Even if we have every intention of saying "no," we tend to go out of our way to soften the blow for the other person, to the point that it sounds to them as though there is room for bargaining.

Manipulative people are well aware of this vulnerability, and they use it to push the envelope as far as it can go. If they detect any hint of hesitation on your part, they take it and run with it; they'll try to guilt-trip you, shame you, threaten you, and do anything else they can think of to turn your "no" into a "yes."

You can try to use diplomatic language wherever it's necessary, but when you say "no" don't leave your statement open to interpretation. For example, if you say, "I don't think I can do it" instead of "I can't do it," a manipulator will take it as a challenge to try and change your mind.

When interacting with manipulators, you also have to learn to assert yourself. Manipulators will use lots of techniques to keep you from voicing your opinion or asserting yourself because they know that if you don't clarify your position, they will be able to co-opt your view and make decisions for you. During the conversation, when you try to make a stand on an issue, the manipulator will attempt to keep you from doing so by talking over you or interrupting you. When this happens, most people will let it go, and the manipulator will get it his way.

When manipulators want you to agree with them inadvertently, they may use "we "sentences to get you to feel like they are on your side, or even to speak for you in front of others. They may also speak in incomplete sentences or ask you to confirm every assertion they make because they are trying to make you more agreeable. To counter ensure that you never let anyone speak for you. Where the manipulator is involved, always make sure that you use "I" statements (e.g., "I want" or "I disagree") to create a clear distinction between you and the manipulator.

Manipulators seek to control others to get them to do what they want. They aim to exploit people by paying with their thoughts and feelings. With this in mind, it's possible to indemnify manipulators by their words, body language, and behavior.

If you meet a person who encourages you to reveal a lot of personal details while at the same time, he is going out of his way to hide details about himself, chances are you are dealing with a manipulator.

You can also tell that you are dealing with a manipulator if the person's actions don't match his words. Manipulators want to win you over, so they'll tell you what they think you want to hear. They'll make lofty promises at first, but when it comes to following through with those promises, they'll leave you hanging. So, pay close attention to what people say and what they do, and try to see if there is a disconnection between those two things.

Manipulators will try to alter your reality and change your belief systems. So, you should watch out for people who tell you blatant lies, even if the facts are easily verifiable. For example, when you are starting to date someone, and you catch them in a lie, but they keep insisting that their version of events is the true one, you can be certain that this is just the beginning, and that over time, their lies will just get more blatant.

Manipulators undermine your grasp on reality by telling constant lies. When you hear small but incremental lies over and over, you

111

will get to a point where you start doubting your reality. In some cases, it can turn out so badly, that you start feeling as though you are losing your mind. This is a manipulation technique that's known as "alighting," and it's more prevalent than you might think.

When you notice that someone is telling obvious lies early in a relationship, your best course of action is to terminate that relationship and to get away from that person as fast as you can.

You can also tell if you are dealing with a manipulator if he or she plays the blame game or tries to make you feel guilty about pretty much everything. Emotional manipulators understand that they can leverage guilt to make people do things for them as a way of atoning for their mistakes. While manipulators may be good at hiding their true nature during the early stages of a relationship, "guilt-tripping" and the "blame game" are two of the things that they find rather difficult to conceal. To manipulators, these techniques are useful from the outset of a relationship, so they may use them without even realizing it themselves.

If something goes wrong on your date, manipulators will try to turn it into your fault, as a matter of record. Even if you are dealing with something that is entirely out of anyone's control, they will make logical leaps to conclude that you are the one to blame. Similarly, if something goes right, they will try to take credit for it. For every small thing that they do, they'll make sure that they point it out, and that you acknowledge that they are the ones who are responsible for it.

For manipulators, the point here is to keep score. From the very beginning of the relationships, they will make sure that there is a running tally of all the good things and the bad things, and they'll make sure that they are ahead on the list of good things, and that you are ahead on the list of bad things. This way, they can always have something to hold over your head in case they want to manipulate you.

So, when you start going out with someone, pay attention to their attitude towards scorekeeping. A scorekeeper is almost always a manipulator.

Manipulators have a way of overwhelming you emotionally, even if you have only known them for a short time. If you meet someone, and you get the sense that they are just "too much too soon," chances are you are dealing with a manipulator.

Love smothering is a common manipulation technique, one that you can detect early in a relationship. Here, the manipulator will shower you with gifts and signs of affection to make you emotionally overwhelmed. When you receive an overwhelming amount of affection, you are more inclined to lead with your heart instead of stopping to think things through, so this increases the chances that you will fall for a manipulator.

Romantic gestures are great at the start of a relationship, but if you feel that they are excessive, you should consider the possibility that you are dealing with a manipulative person.

COMBATTING MANIPULATION

Fighting off manipulative tactics and advances is more than just being able to identify it. Sure, it helps to know that you are being manipulated whenever that truly is the case. That means that you aren't being naive about your situation. However, it's also just as important that you can know the common tactics in dealing with people who seek to manipulate you for their gain.

You've already been exposed to the many faces of manipulation and the kind of impact that it can have on not just one, but on a large group of people. Now, you have to learn how you would be able to spot manipulative behavior in your everyday life. In addition to that, you have to know how you will deal with it whenever you find yourself in those situations as well. It's not rare for people to find themselves in manipulative situations and not know what to do about it. This is not by accident. Manipulative people have a way of compromising their victims' inhibitions and better judgment. That's why a lot of victims of manipulation can often feel paralyzed by the situations that they find themselves in.

If you know that you are in danger of being manipulated, then you need to do something about it. The will to act is entirely up to you.

Chapter 10:

Dealing With Controlling People

HOW TO DEAL WITH A MANIPULATIVE PERSON

Psychological manipulation is always going to be a very loaded and heavy-handed issue. It can often be referred to as lying, deceiving, skewing, distorting, gaslighting, intimidating, guilting, and other such things. Manipulators can also take the form of many different people throughout your life. Sometimes, the person who is manipulating you might be a parent, sibling, boss, classmate, coworker, or romantic partner, among others. That's why manipulation is such a complex topic to handle.

It can take the form of various tactics, and it can also be employed by various agents. This is why it can be increasingly difficult for someone to be able to identify and deal with a manipulative person.

As long as you keep your eyes peeled and you make an active effort in seeking these red flags out, it shouldn't be a problem. Now, it's a matter of dealing with these people and managing their advances.

First, evaluate whether the person is more of a systematic or unconscious manipulator. The more systematic, profound manipulators are almost certainly beyond reach. They can have grand visions and don't care who they have to get by to pursue their goals, they may simply enjoy controlling others.Perhaps they have had childhood traumas and issues that lead them to exploit others for fulfillment. These types of people are more aware of it and aggressively pursue their manipulative traits. Whatever the case may be, if possible, keep your distance from these types of people. Indeed, the easy solution would be to cut this person out of your life, right? It can be so easy to just burn bridges with someone if you know that they have manipulative tendencies and that they would be so willing to advance their interests at your expense. That kind of selfishness should warrant a cutting of ties. However, it's not always going to be that simple. There will be times when the person who is manipulating you is someone you have a deep bond and connection with. There is even a chance they are not consciously aware of their behavior themselves. For instance, if your parent, partner, or friend is manipulating you, it won't be so easy to just break that relationship off entirely. This is especially true if you love your parents and you know that they love you in return. In this case, it's not just a matter of eliminating a manipulative person from your life. Rather, it becomes an issue of managing this individual.

When dealing with a manipulative person, you must tread lightly. Keep in mind that there is also a paternal kind of manipulation.

They might not have bad intentions, and they might take offense to the fact that you are accusing them of being manipulative. That is why you have to be extra cautious and sensitive when you broach the issue with them.

FIRST, BE SAFE

If you know that you are in danger whenever you are with this manipulative individual in your life, always make sure that there is a third-party present. You can never really know what they might do to you if the two of you are alone. So, before you confront them about your manipulation, make sure that you have someone else in the room. You need that mediator; someone who would be able to help bridge the two of you. You can always call on a mutual friend, a shared loved one, or a trusted confidante. In more serious cases, you can even seek professional help from a licensed therapist. The point here is that the confrontation process should never be conducted recklessly. Your safety is always going to be the priority here and a lot of the time, that means having someone else in the room to be with you.

TAKE A DIPLOMATIC APPROACH TO INITIATING A DIALOGUE

You can either choose to work your influence on them to lessen the negative effects, or you could just confront them. The initial confrontation doesn't have to be so hot and impassioned. The best approach to confronting this individual would be to be as calm and collected as can be. You want to make sure that you are taking emotions out of the equation here. Keep in mind that a manipulative person is always going to capitalize on the emotionality of a person. If you take that ammo away from them, then it leaves them very little to work with. In addition to that, it's more likely that they won't react in such a hostile manner if you take a more civil approach to initiating this dialogue with them. Using people's own words against them makes it harder to resist whatever it is you are asking them to do, if one claims to be selfless, then they would not partake in certain actions to begin with.

DON'T FIGHT BACK

If they will be hostile with you about it, resist the urge to fight back. You have to learn to pick your fights. Responding to them in a hostile manner is only going to result in you playing into their games. You don't want that. You want to make sure that you stay calm throughout. When they get emotional, don't invalidate these feelings. Their emotions might be very authentic regardless of whether they are based on distorted truths or not. A person can still feel angry about something that is a complete lie or fantasy. Keep that in mind.

SET CLEAR LIMITS AND BOUNDARIES

Once you have heard their side of the tale, it's now time for you to air out your grievances.

Again, you need to make sure that you keep emotions out of it. You don't want them to be invalidating what you're saying just because you're being hysterical. You want to be honest about it and be straightforward. You shouldn't be beating around the bush anymore.

Make sure that all of the skeletons come out of the closet. Be courteous, but also, don't pull any punches. No matter how uncomfortable it might be to speak honestly about your feelings, you will have to do so.

KNOW WHEN IT'S TIME TO WALK AWAY

Sometimes, you just need to be able to know when it's time to walk away. No matter how painful it is to cut yourself loose from someone who you love dearly, you still have to do so for the sake of your well-being. You should not be making any room for toxicity or manipulative behavior that causes a burden in your life, regardless of who it might be coming from. At the end of the day, the only real person who has your back is yourself. That is why you have to make it a point to protect yourself at all costs. If there is no way for you to find a peaceful means of coexisting with one another that doesn't involve any form of harmful manipulation that is taking value out of your life, then you need to be able to walk away from that.

SEEK APOLOGY FOR YOUR PART AND MOVE ON

You probably won't get an apology, but you also don't have to dwell on it. Own up to what you think you were doing, and then say nothing of the other allegations.

YOU DON'T HAVE TO BEAT THEM

There should be no two people playing this game. Instead, learn to recognize the techniques so that you can practice your responses properly.

KNOW YOUR BASIC HUMAN RIGHTS

In interacting with a psychologically manipulative individual, the most critical rule is to know your rights and understand when they are violated. You have the right to defend yourself until you harm others. On the other hand, you can forfeit those rights if you hurt others.

These are some of our basic human rights:

• You are entitled to be treated with dignity.

• You have the right to have your thoughts, views, and desires shared.

• You are entitled to set your own goals.

- You are entitled to say "no" without feeling guilty. You are entitled to get what you pay for.

- You have the freedom to have differing opinions than others.

- You have the right to care for yourself and to protect yourself against being physically, mentally, or emotionally threatened.

- You are entitled to build your own healthy and happy life.

Those basic human rights are your boundaries.

The culture is, of course, full of people who do not respect those rights. Psychological manipulators want to strip you of your freedoms, so they can take advantage of you and manipulate you. But you have the moral authority and power to announce it is you who is in charge of your life, not the manipulator.

AVOID SELF-BLAME AND PERSONALIZATION

Since the purpose of the manipulator is to try and manipulate your vulnerabilities, it is recognizable that you may feel bad, or even blame yourself for failing to satisfy the manipulator. It is important to remember that you are not the problem in these situations; you have been manipulated to feel bad about yourself so that you are more likely to surrender your power and rights.

BY PROBING QUESTIONS, YOU PUT FOCUS ON THEM

Psychological manipulators will inevitably make demands (or requests) of you. Often these "offers" make you be out of your route to satisfy their needs. When you hear an unreasonable request, it is sometimes useful to put the focus back on the manipulator by asking a few inquiring questions, to see if she or he has enough self-awareness to recognize their scheme's inequity. For instance: "Does that seem fair to you?""Sound fair what you want from me?" "Have I got a say in this?" "Are you asking me, or are you telling me?"

"So, what am I going to get out of it?" "Do you expect me to [re-establish the unjust request]?"You're putting up a mirror when you ask such questions so that the manipulator can see the true nature of his or her plan. If the manipulator has some sense of self-awareness, he or she will likely withdraw the demand and return. On the other side, genuinely pathological manipulators (such as a narcissist) will ignore your questions and convince you to get their way.

A "No" IS A COMPLETE SENTENCE

Practicing the art of communication is to be able to say "no" diplomatically but firmly. Articulated efficiently, it lets you stand your ground while keeping a relationship. Remember that your basic human rights include the right to emphasize yourself, the right to say "no" without feeling shame, and the right to choose your own happy and healthy life.

TAKE TIME FOR YOUR ADVANTAGE

In addition to unreasonable demands, the manipulator will also often expect an immediate response from you to enhance their power and influence over you in the situation.

During these times, instead of instantly reacting to the manipulator's appeal, consider taking time to your benefit and distancing yourself from its immediate impact. You can exercise control over the situation simply by saying: "I'll think about it." Remember how powerful those few words are from a buyer to a salesperson, or from a romantic prospect to an enthusiastic pursuer, or from you to a manipulator.

Take the time you need to weigh the pros and cons of a situation and decide whether you want to discuss a fairer deal, or whether you're better off by saying"no," which brings us to our next point.

CONFRONT BULLIES

The critical point to remember about bullies is that they choose those they view as weaker, so as long as you stay calm and obedient, you become a target for them. However, inside a lot of bullies are also cowards. Once their victims start showing backbone and sticking up for their rights, the bully always backs down. This is true in schoolyards, in households, and offices as well.

YOU CAN SET BOUNDARIES

• When a manipulative person becomes aware that they are losing control, their tactics can become more desperate. It is time to make some tough choices.

• If you don't need to be close to that person, consider cutting them off entirely from your life.

• If you're living with them or working closely together, you'll need to learn strategies to handle them.

• Speaking to a therapist or counselor about how to handle the situation might be helpful.

• You may also be able to recruit a trusted friend or family member to help you identify the activity and impose limits.

SET CONSEQUENCES

If a psychological manipulator persists on breaching the limits and won't take "no" for a response, the outcome will be deployed. One of the essential skills you can use to "stand up" to a stubborn person is the ability to identify and demonstrate consequence(s). Expertly formulated, the outcome gives the deceptive person a pause and compels him or her to move from abuse to respect.

Chapter 11:

Defending Yourself Against Manipulation

WHAT YOU NEED TO DO TO OVERCOME MANIPULATION

We have come to a point where we are here to talk about the basic skills to overcome manipulation. Moreover, manipulation will only work if you allow them to control you. Much like hypnosis, any hypnosis is self-hypnosis. What we are trying to state here is that knowledge that you are being manipulated defeats its entire purpose.

ESTABLISH A CLEAR SENSE OF SELF

There is a need to know your identity, what your needs and wants are, what your emotions are, and what you are fond of and not fond of. You must learn to accept these and not become apologetic, as these are the things that make you, you. At times, we dread that in the event of speaking up, we are viewed by others as egotistical and called out for being selfish. Nevertheless, knowing your identity or what you need in life is not at all an act of selfishness. Self-centeredness is demanding that you always get what you want or that others have always put your needs and wants first. Similarly, when another person calls you out for not following their orders or fulfilling their needs and wants, they are the ones being selfish, not you.

SAY "NO" DESPITE THE OTHER PERSON'S DISAPPROVAL

The ability to say "no" despite somebody's objection is a solid demonstration. Individuals who can do this are present in reality. Because in reality, there is no way that we can accommodate all of their needs and wants.

When this happens, they will become baffled, even disappointed. However, keep in mind that what they are feeling is part of human nature.

Most of these individuals would then forgive and forget. Sound individuals realize that getting what you want all the time is not possible, even when the desires are genuine. In any case, when we cannot endure another person's mistake or objection, it ends up hard stating "no." It winds up more diligently for us to state it or have limits. Manipulators exploit this shortcoming and use dissatisfaction and objection in extraordinary structures to get us to do what they need.

125

TOLERATE THE OTHER PERSON'S NEGATIVE AFFECT

We can demonstrate compassion for people's pity, hurt, or even annoyance when accommodating them without needing to back down and reverse our decision. Keep in mind, a solid relationship is described by common minding, shared genuineness, and shared regard. If you are involved with somebody who uses manipulation and unhealthy control consistently, begin to see little propensities that may not be clear to you at first.

KEEP A CONVERSATIONS JOURNAL

There are usually some kinds of signs that send hints that somebody is trying to manipulate them.

Those aren't always easy to find, of course, unless you've been in the situation before or recognize coercion. One strategy that you can do if you feel you are being manipulated by someone is to keep a journal of what's said. You can write down your conversations or stuff they say to you randomly.

You should even write down what they are doing at the same time. Although this may sound like an unusual thing to do, it will help you understand what is happening, since manipulators are operating on an emotional level.

This is sometimes hard to notice, especially if you are already lacking in self-confidence. You may also include how the mentioned circumstance or words made you feel. You may find a connection between what is stated by the manipulator and how you feel.

You might find, for example, that your self-image is starting to diminish. When you notice this, it is a sign that you have to stay away from the person or get out of the relationship as quickly as possible.

CONFRONTING MANIPULATORS ABOUT THEIR CONDUCT

With some people, that will be easier than others. For example, if your supervisor is the manipulator, and you need your job, you may not be able to confront them directly. You might also have a hard time confronting your significant other, especially if they've lowered your self-esteem. Confronting the manipulator, however, is a perfect way to let them know you understand their actions and you won't stand for it. When you are following this path, you want to be aware of the other tactics that they may be used against you. They might try to create a distraction, for example, or try to play the victim. They might also blame someone else for their behavior or tell you that you imagined it all. You need to be firm when confronting a manipulator. You need to be fully persuaded and understand that they will try and exploit you because they don't want other people to catch on to their actions. You also need to be careful, as some manipulators can become passive-aggressive or violent.

PUT THE FOCUS OF THE MANIPULATORS

You can also focus on themanipulator, in addition to confronting them. You can do this by asking a range of questions regarding their motive. You want to try and find out why they act the way they do, which is the foundation of dark psychology. Some of the questions you may ask are: "Do you feel reasonable?" "What will I get out of this?" "Is this helpful?" "That's what you want from me (state their request)." You show the manipulator what they are doing by asking questions like these. They would be remorseful or alter their request if they are not a master manipulator and did not intend to take part in that action. If they're a master manipulator, however, they'll think of other tactics to turn it back on you. They will try to act like the victim, by asking "Why are you attacking me?"or by saying "I'm just trying to help; I don't appreciate being attacked like this."

127

START DRIVING YOUR AGENDA

Manipulators don't want to win over other people. This puts them in a threatened position. The more you succeed, though, the more you drive a manipulator backward. Your ability to believe in and continue to succeed in yourself will depend on how long you know the manipulator and how close you are to them. For example, if you have been emotionally beaten down by the manipulator, it will be much harder to remain motivated and work hard to succeed. If you've just met them, without too much trouble you'll be able to continue pushing towards your success. Of course, having the mindset of believing that you can fulfill your dreams, and supporting people will help eliminate the manipulator through your success. And if you need to speak to someone to get better mentally and emotionally, this is what you do.

DON'T GET PHYSICALLY TIED UP

While sometimes we get trapped by a manipulator because we don't know their personality, other times we know they're manipulators, but they still need to keep in touch because they're colleagues or family. You need to protect yourself in a different way when this is the situation because you cannot simply ignore them. A lot of people also recommend you do your best not to get emotionally attached. For some people, this will be tougher than others. If you're a more emotional person, you'll be struggling to avoid becoming emotionally attached as your relationships are emotionally based.

One way to do this is to ensure that they know the boundaries. You'll also need to make sure that you stick to your limits. If you cross your boundaries, manipulators don't care, so you need to protect yourself. Tell them if you think they're jumping a fence. Don't fall back for any of their techniques and don't turn back.

DON'T FEED THE DRAMA

One of the most essential things a manipulator thrives on is suspense. For this reason, they often disagree with someone or something that will cause people to respond. So one of the best ways to stop a manipulator in their tracks is to tell them "you are right." Manipulators aren't used to having people to agree with them, and when you do, they'll be left speechless. This also creates a threat that could make them want to leave you alone. They may feel that they can't trap you with their techniques, especially if you do so right away. This is not to say that they will not try. Manipulators also aim to bring people into the network. Letting them win the argument, even if it upsets your ego a little bit, is much better than falling victim to their pitfalls.

HAVE A HEALTHY ATTITUDE

Having a healthy mindset is another way of eliminating a manipulator from your life. You want to make sure you feel confident that you can stop them from using techniques against you. You will want to make sure you feel good about your self-esteem and self-image. At the same time, you want to understand how they manipulate you.

To battle them, you need to have a grasp on their techniques. You have to understand they probably won't stop with just one technique. More than likely they will use a few in hopes they can start breaking you down.

The stronger you remain, the more likely the manipulator will leave you alone.

If you always push them away, call them out on their behavior, and continue to believe in yourself, manipulators won't spend a lot of time trying to use different techniques.

MEDITATION

Many people don't realize how helpful meditation can be. Meditation is not just about keeping you relaxed but also about keeping you optimistic and feeling good about yourself. When you feel this way, it's easier to remove the negativity from your life, which means manipulators. Meditation is easy, so you don't have to put too much time aside. You can schedule meditation in around ten minutes out of your day. Find a time and place where you can be on your own and without interruption. You also want to keep it quiet, so you can concentrate on eliminating your body and mind from the negativity. Many people would be using relaxation exercises to help them remain focused when meditating. This is when you close your eyes and start to breathe normally. You want to concentrate on the breaths. Notice the feeling of your body on your clothes or put one hand on your chest and the other on your stomach. Feel how your hands move in and out as you breathe. Then you focus on deep breaths. Take a deep breath in, then slowly exhale. Finish the exercise until you feel soothed.

In addition to helping you eliminate manipulators who have not become a close person in your life, meditation will also help you manage your life with a manipulator. Of course, if your significant other is a manipulator for your mental health and safety, you want to leave but meditation can help give you strength. It will give you the strength to concentrate on your attitude and find ways to defend yourself against the tactics of coercion. It may give you the strength to leave as well, once you're ready.

ASEPSIS AND TOTAL AVOIDANCE

That is, do not get close to a handler, to avoid contact and contagion as much as possible. Of all the strategies, this is the most effective. It's not the most epic, but it does work the best. The first security strategy in any situation is always avoidance. The basic strategy for winning a battle with a manipulator is not to enter the battle. That is the only correct maneuver because any other way has consequences.

"A manipulator is an expert in fighting in the mud, from behind, and with low blows, he will win against us if we go down to his ground."

In bad times, both personal and business, there is a temptation to listen to more dubious clients, frequently worse companies, fall into "get rich effortlessly" or "it's always someone else's fault" schemes (so better end with them). We have to avoid that as much as possible; we have to leave them alone and put a bell of silence on the manipulator.

It is far better to miss an "opportunity" to work with a manipulator than to get bogged down with one. Nobody goes around exposing themselves to the flu just to show how strong they are. Our primary strategy with disease and with manipulation should be the same: do not enter their radius of action as far as possible.

CUT THE ROPE AT ONCE, AS SOON AS POSSIBLE

The former is the best strategy, but it is impossible to avoid 100% manipulation. Sometimes they will catch us off guard and, at other times, circumstances will drag us into a situation, whether we like it or not. There will also be times when it will be friends, family, or acquaintances who will be in a manipulative situation and we will have to get involved to help them.

"In these circumstances, and from experience, the appropriate strategy is to cut ties with the manipulator as soon as possible. We will do it quickly as if it were a clean blow of the sword. Then we take as much distance as possible."

I know it may seem suggestive to be the vigilante and believe that we will not be fooled but resist the temptation. Every minute that you spend with a manipulator, you will be draining precious energy. If we are there, the strategy is to disengage from the fight as soon as possible, "hit" only to gain distance, and then avoid further contact in the future.

If you are involved in business with a manipulator, terminate any contracts, say no to the slightest bit that you propose, seek outside support, and do not isolate yourself by listening only to the manipulator.

NEVER DIRECTLY CONFRONT A MANIPULATOR IF YOU CAN AVOID IT

If he does, he will flee by other roads, mount the number, play the victim, or use one of his hat's many tricks. We have to be smarter than them.

"If you spot a manipulator, don't go straight for it, look for an indirect angle, and strike with one of the following strategies to break away from their influence and distance yourself."

I repeat, do not go to direct war.

NEVER, NEVER, LOSE YOUR TEMPER

As the Americans say: "Business is business."This phrase alludes to a philosophy whereby there is no reason for the emotional to get in the way of business. With that mentality of separating the professional from the personal, many businesses take some huge (business) stab wounds and solve them with, "It's just business."

"The exercise to be learned is that, in business and against manipulation, you never lose your temper."

If emotion surfaces, the manipulator wins. If he fails, he begins to despair, uses more violent tactics, exposes himself, makes mistakes, discovers his game, and loses the ability to manipulate.

132

The manipulator seeks the brawl, and if the other loses the papers, we have to turn it around and use that strategy against him. We must know that we are winning every second that we do not lose our temper and do not get carried away by emotion.

Never get upset by a manipulator, be it in a personal or professional situation. Let's see the situation for what it is, a surgical operation to remove it from our environment, and not do more damage. It will twist, scream, and kick, getting louder and dirtier, like when little children get angry. But if we hold the guy, he loses.

LEARN TO INTERPRET THE SIGNALS.

It is vital to recognize a manipulator and be aware of our emotional state in a negotiation, sale, or discussion with one.

The four main clues that should set off the alarms because we are in front of a professional liar are:

INSULATION

Trying to isolate ourselves in a conversation, a situation, or somethingthat we do not consult or talk about with others, are signs of manipulation.

Isolation is a typical manipulative tactic that is imperative, such as for cults, to make them work. Any sensible person who proposes something to us has no problem in consulting other opinions.

RUSH AND PRESSURE

When someone tries to get us to rashly buy a product, sign a contract, make any decision, or go out of business, something stinks. You have to distance yourself, consult other options, and decide calmly. "We should never make an important decision in a hurry or an upset, emotional state."

EXCESS OF EMOTIONS

Be careful when an excess of emotionality is used in the speeches, they make us or the situations they put us in, easier to manipulate. I have seen firsthand how certain unethical companies in the field of self-help act, for example.

They organize weekends where attendees are isolated in a hotel or spa; they are put in an altered and highly elevated emotional state (with exercises, practices, and speeches that strike a chord).

Then all this is used to sell more expensive programs and courses, of course, in a rush and pressure using a false shortage (another typical manipulation trick). "If you can put someone in a sufficiently upset emotional state, you can make them believe what you want."

EXCESS "LOVE" AND ATTENTION

One of the cults' preferred strategies for attracting followers is called the "love bomb." It is characterized because everyone accepts you unconditionally, smiles at you, and behaves like the best thing that ever happened to them, even though they hardly know you. There is no criticism; no one says no to anything, it's all gestures and acceptance smiles.

Acceptance is a harsh drug for anyone, but especially for those who have barely been able to obtain it, such as the lonely, the marginalized, or those going through a hard time. Those can all be us, and those are the scapegoats.

We can all fall into the "love bomb." Likewise, the lack of seriousness, the excess confidence, the refusal to sign contracts or agreements because everyone here "are friends"... All of these are usually signs of manipulation.

IF IN DOUBT, ALSO SAY THAT YOU WANT TO GET A SECOND OPINION TO SEE THE MANIPULATOR'S REACTION.

Similar to the previous time strategy, in this case, we say we want a second opinion. Even when we are responsible for the decision to be made, we can always say that we must consult someone else: a lawyer, our spouse, a friend who is an expert on the subject.

It is about trying to get out of the isolation trap with arguments that are difficult to refute. A desperate effort on the other not to consult a superior or an expert is a sign that we are possibly being manipulated. These two strategies work as a detector for manipulators and differentiate them directly in a delicate situation.

DO NOT GIVE IN TO A MANIPULATOR OR IN THE MOST INOFFENSIVE DETAILS

If you think you are dealing with a manipulator, don't say yes to anything. No matter how innocent he seems. If we do, we are at risk of using cognitive dissonance (one of the fundamental principles of persuasion) to make us take a seemingly simple step and then gradually get more agreement from our part. When we realize it, it has pushed us to the bottom of the web.

If you know you are involved with a manipulator, never get closer than necessary, never say yes and never think you have everything under control. It must be noted that often and we are not obliged to justify this refusal, we are within our rights, and "no" is a complete sentence.

If he insists, we say the same,"no"; we do not add additional excuses that he can grab on to. Manipulators are adept at emotional blackmail and trying to get excuses to see how to turn them around.

BE VERY CLEAR ABOUT THE INITIAL OBJECTIVE YOU HAVE IN MIND

This is the first golden rule of negotiation, but it should be remembered for any situation in which we interact with a manipulator.

"If your objective in the conversation or negotiation with a manipulator is vague and diffused, you will end up at a point that the manipulator wants."

Be very clear about what you want. Never confront a manipulator without knowing precisely what you want to get out of the interaction. If you will cut the ties with the manipulator, focus everything on reducing the links and not moving from there. If you want to hear what he has to say and then reflect ahead of time, with other opinions and without pressure, keep that in mind and don't allow anything else to happen.

Listen to him, and don't let the manipulator get to anything other than the goal you have in mind. Since this is the real world, you should have an ideal target in mind and then a realistic goal, being prepared to compromise (though not quickly) from that ideal goal to the actual one. However, that is the minimum limit, do not give another step.

Know your destiny, as far as you can give in, and then be like Ulysses returning from Troy. Hold on tight to your targets and resist any manipulative siren calls.

NEVER USE THE SAME WEAPONS AS A MANIPULATOR

There is a powerful temptation to use weapons of manipulation against the manipulator. To respond with fallacies, try to isolate him, do emotional blackmail, or put on an act ourselves to increase that emotion in the situation. "Don't fall for it, because they are based on lies, which has practical consequences. I do not want to sound like a preacher, but they never come out for free."

There is a red line that delimits persuasion, and on the other side are manipulation techniques. The first few times, this line commands respect, and it is difficult to cross it. But when we've crossed it the first time and have fallen into unethical manipulation, the line is blurred even for a legitimate purpose. That way, it is much easier to transfer it again a second time.

Do it a few more times, and the line will be erased, and we will have become one of them.

But it is also that manipulation is not necessary. There is a large amount of material on ethical persuasion to learn; you can use scarcity without isolating or pressing; you can use cognitive dissonance without it being a trap to fleece a victim. Always remember to have ethics, because if there is one thing I have learned, it is that manipulators do not end up well.

ACT QUICKLY

It's great that you have come to terms with the reality of things, but defense against these dark manipulative tactics entail so much more. Attempting to defend yourself from the claws of these manipulators, is often intense and exhilarating at first.

This intensity of these emotions may cause one to slowly slide into denial. The more you delay in taking any action, that is usually what accelerates the onset of this denial, and when it happens, there are high chances that you might relapse and end up getting trapped in the same web.

This can be avoided by taking action immediately when you realize that someone is trying to manipulate you. This can present itself in the simplest of ways, like when informing a close friend of the reality of a particular situation may be all that's needed so set in motion a series of events that will eventually lead to your freedom.

You should know that the fabric of illusion is made from a tougher material than glass after choosing to act. The illusion could work its way back into your heart with your emotions in high gear by using fragments of your emotions to fix it.

When a liar is caught in a lie, he or she may attempt to recruit others to enforce that lie when they feel that they are no longer holding you.

A deceptive partner with whom you have recently broken things off, would at this point try to use the other mutual relationships in your life to change your mind.

If you want to get out of this unscathed, you will need both your logic and instincts. Although the truth of the situation is that when you discover that you've been lied to consistently, you become emotionally scarred, so the issue of leaving the situation unscathed becomes unlikely.

Priority should be given, however, to take the route that allows you to leave this toxic situation without harming yourself further. You're all over the place emotionally. Rage, anger, hurt, and deception is the tip of the iceberg, but logically, you need to think. Keep your head above the water and warn yourself.

TRUST YOUR INSTINCTS

While your brain interprets signals based on facts, logic, and sometimes experience, your heart works in the opposite direction by screening information through an emotional filter. The only thing that picks up vibrations is your gut instinct, which neither the heart nor the brain can pick on.

If you can groom yourself to the point where you recognize your inner voice and are trained to react to it, you will lower your chances of being seduced by people trying to work on you with their manipulative will.

To begin, it's hard to recognize this voice. That's because we allowed voices of doubt, self-discrimination as well as the critics' loud voices within to be heard and without drawing out our authentic voice throughout our lives.

Your survival depends on this voice or instinct. So, trust that when it kicks in, your brain neurons can still process things in your immediate vicinity.

Some people call it intuition, and some refer to it as instinct, especially when it comes to relationships, they are undoubtedly the same thing. You must accept that it may not always make logical sense to start trusting your instincts.

If you've ever been in the middle of doing something and experienced the feeling of being watched all of a sudden, then you know what I mean. You don't have eyes at the back of your head, there's no one else with you in the room, but you get that tiny shiver running down your spine and the "sudden knowledge" that you're being watched. That's what I'm talking about.

The first step to connect with your instinct is to decode your mind with the voices you've let in. With meditation, you can do this. Forget the chatter of "he said, she said." Concentrate on your center. You are the voice you know. Next, be careful about your thoughts. Don't just throw away the eclectic monologue in your head. Rather go with the flow of thoughts.

Why do you think of a certain person in some way? How do you feel so deeply about this person, even if you only know each other for a few days? What's that nagging feeling about this other person that you have? You get more tuned to your intuition as you explore your thoughts and understand when your instincts kick in and how to react to it.

You may need to learn to take a step back to pause and think if you are the kind of person who prefers to make decisions in the spur of the moment.

This moment in which you pause, allows you to reflect on your decisions and evaluate them. The next part is hard, and it couldn't be followed by many people. Unfortunately, you can't skip or navigate around this step.

This part has to do with trust. You need to be open to the idea of trusting yourself and trusting others to be able to trust your instinct. Your failure to trust others would just make you paranoid, and it's not your instincts that kick in when you're paranoid.

It's the fear in you. Fear tends to turn every molehill into a mountain. You must let go of your fear, embrace confidence, and let that lead in your new relationships.

You are better able to hear the voice inside without the roadblocks put up by fear in your mind. Finally, your priorities need to be reevaluated.

If your mind is at the forefront of money and material possessions, you may not be able to see the past. Any interaction you have with people would be interpreted as people trying to take advantage of you, and if you dwell on that frequently enough, it will soon become your reality.

You attract into your life what you think of. If you're constantly thinking about material wealth, you're only going to attract people who think like you. Using this as a guide, look at all your relationships with this new hindsight; the old, the new, and the prospective.

Don't enter a relationship that expects to be played. Be open when you approach them, whether it's a business relationship, a romantic relationship, or even a regular acquaintance. You can get the right feedback about them from your intuition.

Do not step into this thinking, too, that your gut will tell you to run in the opposite direction when you meet suspect people.

HOW TO CONFRONT A BULLY SAFELY

Not all manipulators resort to bullying, but many of them do. Someone is being a bully when they use intimidation or harm to get what they want from you. Always remember, that a bully chooses people they see as weak to pick on, and compliance and passivity will only strengthen this. However, a lot of bullies are afraid and insecure deep down, so when their victim starts to stand up for themselves, this will often lead the bully to back off. Whether this situation is occurring in a playground or at the office, it applies, most of the time. Keep in mind that many bullies have withstood bullying and violence. Although this doesn't excuse their behaviors, it does help the victim to understand.

YOUR INFLUENCE SKILL SET

CLARITY OF PURPOSE

An important facet of the ability to influence others is your clarity. Know what you want and have a clear plan of how you will get it. Whether you're working in sales and trying to improve the team's quarterly figures or trying to encourage a student to be more diligent with study, or to set them on a career path – know what the objective is. The only way you can succeed in influencing someone to behave in a desired way is if you are clear about what you hope to achieve. You don't get in your car to drive to a destination you've never been without setting the GPS. The same goes for the application of influence toward achieving a desired effect or goal. Know where you're going.

Always be prepared in advance, with the following:

A list of prioritized objectives.

A clear picture of the final destination (what it looks like).

Preparing the environment.

If you are seeking to reach an agreement with someone, you need to make them feel comfortable. You also need to be relaxed and yourself. At the same time, for effective communication (which is important when you want to influence someone's behavior, as this book is explaining) you need to make the environment conducive to your interaction. You need to have in place a planned sequence of events at that meeting beforehand.

The best way to achieve this is to draw up a meeting agenda and circulate it to those who will attend, one day before the meeting. In this way, everyone knows what to expect and what shape the meeting will take. The agenda should make clear what the goals of the meeting are. Checking off the items on it should move you closer to the agreement, if not enable all present to reach consensus to move forward. The logical sequence of events represented by following an agenda is a function of a critically structured plan. Having a plan of such quality never fails to impress.

CONSENSUS BUILDING

In building consensus, you're making it clear you are open to suggestions (which you should always be, regardless of your single-minded focus on your ultimate goal). Hearing what people say and truly listening means you're not planning a response while they're talking. It means you're actively hearing everything they say. Subtext, word choice, and tone are all important and so are your skills at hearing what's being said. Proceeding with these skills in play can provide you with the basis for genuine and not false consensus.

False consensus is reached when people are "heard out", but not "heard". These are two entirely different animals. The first is the condescending indulgence of hearing what no longer matters because a decision has already been made and the results of that decision, imposed. Being heard means that influence on the final decision is still a possibility and that what's offered may result in concessions, if it features actual merit.

Being present to the input of others and being able to integrate their thoughts and suggestions into an existing plan is a function of leadership. Leadership is not imposed. Leadership is extended to others as a service. Consensus building is a way to bring forward the knowledge of the team and add it to your own. In the case of reaching an agreement, it's the foundation of lasting relationships that won't later be ruptured by objections to not being heard. This is extremely important. Autocratic leadership is unwelcome and will not survive for long. It is a corrosive leadership style that is not sustainable.

CREATING RAPPORT

When someone begins to enjoy your company, it becomes much easier for you to enlist their support. This makes it more likely they'll support your viewpoint in situations in which it counts. Allies are people who like and trust you. Your relationships are what will move your goals forward and create a foundation for your success and that of your allies. People, while perhaps not being entirely aware of this on an intellectual level, know this instinctively. That is

143

why you must prioritize establishing rapport with others. It's the basis of strong allegiances.

Part of creating rapport is establishing the common interests you hold with others. Taking an interest in them and offering them information about who you are is how this is achieved. Being too veiled about yourself makes you appear cold, calculating, and detached. Establish that you're open and also, a person who can be trusted.

It's also important to establish easily with others and one way this can be done is to mirror the body language. You'll probably find (if you pay attention), that you do this anyway when you've begun to establish rapport with someone. Mirroring body language sends the unconscious signal that there is a bond already established between two people and that they're on the same team. Mirroring speech patterns is another way of doing this. Repeating keywords with enthusiasm at opportune times is another natural way we tell each other we're enjoying a conversation or agreeing with each other. Nod, smile, and respond positively when you sense a common theme emerging in conversation. This sends the message that you're accessible on the most basic, human level.

SUGGESTIONS INSTEAD OF DEMANDS

People routinely bridle at directives. In Western societies where individualism is a way of life, we like to believe in our autonomy as a value. That means it's not the best course of action to demand things from people. Much more effective is suggesting a course of action and building consensus based on the suggestion while being open to input and concessions to other points of view. This is the democratic way of achieving goals and one that is completely manageable with the application of a deft hand.

Here are examples of language that gives your listener the option to chip in and yet still leaves you the "wiggle room" to get to where you believe you need to go:

"Would you be interested in doing a-b-c?"

"Could you be interested in doing a-b-c?"

"I think we should do a-b-c. What do you think?"

"Do you think this is the best way forward, or do you have other ideas?"

Leaving space for opinion and input, while still advancing the validity of your own opinion is the stuff of which influence is made. While you're providing people with a rationale for your point of view, your willingness to entertain amendments to that point of view only increases your influential power. Imposition rarely ends in anything but resentment. By building consensus through input and exchange, you will still arrive at the goal you have in mind, but you'll do it with the support of a willing team, signed on to the plan in question. A fringe benefit? That input will undoubtedly improve on the original plan and will result in satisfaction on the part of all involved.

HEIGHTENING YOUR AWARENESS

Awareness of the responses of other people to what you're saying is key to influential action. What are their facial expressions telling you? Their body language and word choices? What about tone and pitch? All these factors are rich with information that you can draw on to temper your pitch and get people on your side. It can also cue you to back off and change lanes, while you re-group and allow others their input.

Active listening, while employing body language (head nodding, eye contact) and assenting noises ("uh-huh", "yes", "I see") is also about deeply engaging with what's being said and the complimentary messages being sent by the speaker. Your awareness in crucial situations, of all the factors that create a communicative environment, is of the utmost importance. You need to be aware, not only of what's being said but implications about what's intended, what's not being said, and the speaker's frame of mind. All these factors work together to form a more concise body of information from which you may draw to apply influential action.

WHAT TO DO IN CASE OF MANIPULATION?

You must also be aware that the manipulator will never change because he does not do it for a specific logical reason that has a right place in real life.He does it because he needs it and this need is dictated by his personality, along with his dark and problematic psychological state; in practice if he does it today then tomorrow he will start looking for reasons to go back to doing it again and again and again and again.

For this reason, a good way to escape manipulation is to remove the manipulator, be it a partner or an employer, a neighbor, or an acquaintance. When this is not possible because there is coexistence with this individual, then we must defend ourselves and a good way to do this is to be aware, as I said before, of the way the manipulator operates and to establish a virtual border between the manipulator and manipulated so that the latter does not feel responsible for all the problems that arise from this "coexistence". In other words, you have to ignore it!

To defend yourself from manipulation you also need to be able to recognize and manage your emotions and your body to understand and accept when you are being manipulated and the traumas that have been suffered. To practice advice on how to defend yourself from manipulation, you must first be able to accept it. Dark manipulation is defined so, primarily, because it is a weapon generally used by psychologically problematic subjects and believe me you can meet one more frequently than you can imagine. Secondly, it is called so because it is manipulation that has purposes that are not enough to be definedas negatives as they are subtle.

HOW TO AVOID BEING NEGATIVELY MANIPULATED BY OTHERS

Be aware of your rights: The absolute most important rule you can follow when dealing with someone who wants to manipulate you in negative ways, is to know your worth and rights. This way, you will always know when someone is attempting to violate them. So long as others are not getting harmed in the process, you should be defending yourself. Every human should have the right to have differing opinions from others, to protect yourself, to say "no" when you need to, and to decide what's important to you. You should also have the right of expressing your wants, opinions, and feelings, and always be treated with respect.

Unfortunately, the world has plenty of people who won't want to acknowledge or respect your rights, especially negative manipulators. You will also come into contact with others who generally wish to take advantage of any opportunity. However, you can proudly defy this by letting them know that you are the one who runs your life, no one else.

Maintain healthy distance: Another way to tell who is manipulative, is to pay attention to the way someone acts in varying situations and in front of various individuals. Although everyone, to a degree, puts on different faces depending on where they are, most people who are harmfully manipulative are extreme about it. They might, for example, be extremely polite and friendly to one person, and

147

completely disrespect another, or act like a victim one second, and then act controlling immediately after.

If you notice someone acting this way regularly, it's a good sign to distance yourself from them and not engage with them unless it's an absolute necessity. Usually, the reasons behind these types of behavior are complicated, and it isn't your duty or responsibility to help or change that person. Trying to do so will often only lead to suffering on your part, so it's better not to expect much when you notice these signs.

Don't blame yourself: A person who wishes to manipulate others in harmful ways searches for weaknesses to exploit, so it makes sense that someone who has been victimized by one might blame themselves or feel inadequate. But in a situation like this, you should remember that it isn't you that's the issue here; you are being pressured to feel bad by someone else who is very good at making people feel bad.

This is how they get their way. Instead, think about the relationship you have with this person and ask yourself if they are respecting you, demanding reasonable things from you, and whether you are both benefiting, or only one of you is. Ask yourself, also, if you feel good about yourself after spending time with this person, or if you would feel better being around them less. The way you answer these questions will lead to important answers about where the issue lies in the situation.

Questioning them: Eventually, this type of person will demand or request things from you. Many times, these requests or others will consider their needs, while completely ignoring yours. Next time you receive a solicitation that is completely unreasonable, turn the focus back to them by asking some questions. Ask them if their request is reasonable, or if what they are asking from you is fair.

You can also try asking if you get to have an opinion in this matter or ask what benefit you will be gaining from the arrangement.

Each time you ask questions like this, you are holding a mirror up to them, allowing them to see what they are truly asking of you. If they are self-aware, they will likely retract their request or demand. But there may be some cases, such as dealing with a narcissist, who will keep insisting without even considering your questions. If that happens, follow these guidelines.

Don't answer Immediately: One way to combat manipulation is to use time as a resource. Often, the manipulator will not only ask you to fulfill an unreasonable demand, but they will want an answer immediately. When this happens, rather than answering right away, use time and distance yourself from their request and influence. This can be done by telling them that you will think about it. Although these words are simple, they give your power back to you, giving you the option to weigh the advantages and disadvantages of the situation and let you work out something better, if need be.

Teach yourself to say "no" when needed: Saying "no" is difficult for many people, since we are often taught and conditioned to be polite whenever possible. Being able to confidently but politely say "no" comes with learning communication skills. When this is articulated effectively, you can hold onto your self-respect, and also continue a healthy relationship. Keep in mind that your rights include deciding what matters to you, being able to turn down a request free from guilt and choosing health and happiness for yourself. You are responsible for your life, not the person who is making unreasonable demands of you.

Create a consequence: Next time a negative manipulator tries to violate your rights, and refuses to accept your answer, set a consequence for their behavior. Knowing how to assert and identify appropriate consequences is a crucial skill for standing down

149

someone who is being very difficult or disrespectful. If you can articulate this clearly and thoroughly, your consequences will cause them to pause and stop violating you, shifting to a position of respect.

Chapter 12:

Protecting Yourself From Manipulation

STRATEGIES FOR PROTECTION AGAINST MANIPULATION

We all love pursuing the other sex every now and then-both men and women. It's fun and a good sport, as long as we're frank about it and bear in mind that it's all about passion. Why? For what? Since it's deceit to try and love cannot be exploited-we don't find love; love finds us. So, we should view a relationship of love as sacred ground.

Sadly, many people believe in deception – both in relationships and in industry. In my early twenties, I read something that stuck for good in my subconsciousness: if you can align yourself with the universe, it's easy to achieve success. What does this mean for this topic? It means manipulations are pointless at the end of the day. Manipulations may potentially offer a short-term benefit, but in the long run, it will eventually lead to consequences as they are opposed by the universe. But if we go with the celestial wind, we'll gravitate toward our target – more or less effortlessly. Too good to be real? Every one of us is playing a part in the cosmic game. In the grand scheme of things, we just have to know our position and let it play out. And Jesus said his cross is as light as a feather. Of course, this means giving up several wishes and aspirations that aren't part of our cameo.However, our celestial intent typically turns out to be much more grandiose than our puny, selfish ambitions.

That being said, we also need to defend ourselves from other people's childish manipulations, including those around us. Don't take this lightly; it's painful, emotional coercion and can leave deep wounds on people's psyche and soul.Once you are in a state of exploitation, it is very difficult to get out. But don't take this affair too seriously, we're doing a lot of things subconsciously, and your partner may not even know that she's manipulating you.

There will always be people trying to shake your trust - people trying to instill seeds of self-doubt inside you. Such people would do their utmost to trick you into thinking that their beliefs are objective facts. They're trying to tell you everyone in the world thinks you're rude, nuts, or not nice. Then they'll tell you how much they're worried about you, how you're living your life, spending your money, raising your children, on and on.

153

If you don't change the way they want you to change, then your life will be destroyed. This is what they want to believe. The truth isyou don't want to help these people. They want to get you under control. We want you to adjust, not to make your life easier, but to affirm their lives and prevent you from overgrowing them.

DON'T GET ANGRY

Manipulative people are not preoccupied with your needs. They worry about their interests. Once you allow manipulative people in your life, it can be extremely difficult to get rid of them. The trick is to have enough self-control to send the boot to dishonest people as soon as you see them. Here are a few ways to get rid of manipulative people from your life:

LISTEN TO YOUR EMOTIONS

when something is wrong, the body sends translatable signals into a sense of general malaise. It is always good to listen to these subliminal messages and try to understand what's wrong.

CHANGE YOUR POINT OF VIEW

If you happen to be in a situation where you feel the stench of manipulation, pretend to be a third person who "observes from outside" what is happening. This is because often we get involved in feelings and we don't judge things for what they are. By following this advice, you can give an objective assessment of the situation.

MAKE IT A REASON

This is easy to understand. You have to understand that manipulation is part of life, such as luck or the sun rising in the morning and setting in the evening. It is something that exists and for which you cannot do anything. On the contrary, you can try to improve and develop your positive side, this will help you a lot.

As for the tactics to be used to defend against a manipulator, having unmasked it, we can say that it will be useful to follow one or more of those listed below:

EXPRESS WHAT YOU DISAGREE WITH

This is because the manipulator criticizes everything, or almost everything, and consequently the victim tries to defend himself in every way to deny it, becoming more and more aggressive (in this case he falls completely into the trap). In this case, the victim only has to express his point of view clearly, calmly, and simply to make the manipulator understand that whatever he says, he will not be able to change his opinion in the least. This will strongly destabilize the manipulator.

ALWAYS SPEAK IN THE FIRST PERSON

Following this simple advice and pretending that the manipulator does the same is important. Many times, the manipulator speaks in third person and remains very vague in expressing his concepts and attacking someone. They never do it directly. This is because his game is to put others in a bad light so that they cannot be accused, because they don't want to "get their hands dirty".

So if you put your back against the wall with phrases like "what do you think of this person" or "what is your opinion on this situation", you are obliged to express yourself directly and take responsibility for it and maybe, feeling "hunted" will make the manipulator take a step back in their path of manipulation.

ACCEPT YOUR MISTAKES

It seems strange but actually, it is an excellent defense strategy, as the manipulator often focuses on feelings of guilt.They do so by trying to steal the victim's secrets, simple facts, or events, even if they are not necessarily serious, and makes sure that they turn against him making her "feel guilty". This applies both to things that happened in the past, to things that happen in the present, and also to things that could happen in the future.

One strategy to annihilate this type of manipulation is to be able to recognize our mistakes if there have been any. At the same time,we should be able to outline our responsibilities, because if it is true that we have made mistakes, it is also true that we cannot take the blame for everythingforever. For example, if a person blames us for our wrong behavior, we can respond by saying sentences like "yes, I made this mistake, but what you say does not concern me", in this case we assume our responsibilities but at the same time we make it clear that in addition to this we are not available to submit to anything else, which makes us appear mature and consequently, not easily manipulated.

SPEAK CALMLY

As mentioned several times in this book, the manipulator prefers emotionally fragile people because he loves to attack the victim's emotions and does not care at all about having a constructive dialogue. By virtue of this, the mistake that many make is that of counterattacking the provocations of the manipulator, which for clarity, is a normal instinctive reaction but in these cases, it is not the right one as he will continue to argueagainst the victim.

It seems absurd but the manipulator is very capable of doing all this. In this case, the defense strategy to be adopted is extremely simple, one only has to recognize that his criticisms are right, never contradict him, and at the same time one must take the right distances in this regard. In practice we can say that you have to make fun of it a bit, using phrases like "I understand your point of view, but I think it's better than ..."

A trick that can help you can replace the term "but" with words like "despite", "nevertheless" "anyway" which according to NLP scholars, would have a "sweeter" but still effective impact.

STRONGLY DENY

When we are confident that what we say is true and we are emotionally strong people, we can also take a more impervious path to defend ourselves from a manipulator and we can deny what he is proposing to us. A dry and firm NO without the use of banal and twisted explanations, perhaps accompanied by an authoritarian body language, will be a good method to desist the manipulator.

Behavioral tone: Having a good behavioral tone is fundamental. It is very similar to a person's emotional intensity, and it is the intensity of one's actions. Don't get the wrong idea because you don't have to scare anyone, it's just about wearing a safe and decisive cover to look like a strong person. If you have or manifest this type of personality, then you will have a good chance that everyone will listen to you because, as the saying goes, actions speak louder than words. This is a good way to be both persuasive and manipulative, so it can also be used as a defense weapon to show the manipulator that you have a strong personality like him and therefore, you are difficult to manipulate.

These tips on how to defend yourself from a manipulator can be applied in multiple cases of manipulation, whether you are dealing with sellers, friends, relatives, employers, people who belong to the religious world, or partners because they are based on the reasoning principles of the manipulator itself and how it works. Keep in mind that manipulative people tend to mask their interests by pretending to help you and then force you to change.It is not to improve your life but so that they can use you, by saying that their opinions, as well as the facts, are the best and yours don't count. They will attract any form of attention and take credit in places where they don't

MANIPULATION AND MIND CONTROL:

deserve it and will do everything, they canto make sure they keep you from escaping. It is worth noting that once they are established in your life, they are difficult to eliminate. This is why I want to remind you again that the best way to defend yourself from manipulation, as many scholars and authorities in the field say, is to escape from it and the manipulator. You only have to deal with it if it is strictly necessary because dealing with a manipulator can become dangerous. In any case, whatever the decision you make, always ask an external person for help, even better if they are qualified.

DON'T FALL INTO THEIR TRAP

Most of us come across instances where others seek to manipulate our thoughts, attitudes, or actions and take advantage of them to their advantage. In one such case, you fail to understand the true motive. The person mentally dominates you, and you step into the pit. Often this emotional abuse costs you a lot when you make some critical decisions under another person's control, and you only realize when it is too late.

You have to be cautious when a relationship sounds too good to be true. They are showering you with compassion, gratitude, admiration, congratulations, and affection. You feel like you live in a dream where everything seems perfect. They don't give you a reason to worry. You simply cannot find any flaws in them. Also, if anything goes wrong, they can begin to weep or feel sorry. You can become the object of extreme intimacy and have passion for the fairy tale.

Because you began the relationship with love bombing, all of a sudden you start feeling ignored. You are receiving gratitude, presents, and recognition, but rarely. You feel like you're losing your grip or want someone else in your life. You get another gift from them, the moment you make up your mind to move on, making the decision difficult. They are trying to get leverage over you in situations like these. For most instances, amazingly, this works, and you end up going back to them

Individuals often succeed in manipulating their victims after intermittent reinforcement. We can avoid behaving in the same way while fighting back or by demanding an answer. The explanation is that they are taking complete care of you now, so there is no need for intermittent strengthening because we no longer need it. Manipulators have many different faces, and in the same manner, they can use many ways to get things done. The person may make a plan, and later deny it, so that you begin to doubt your perception. They make you feel bad when you try to make them aware of their promise. They can employ shallow sympathy and burst into crocodile tears. Eventually, you end up trusting them and even doubting whether you listened correctly.

You can't believe the smiling faces that seem confident and strong are the same manipulative people, that often have self-serving prejudices, so they think less ofother person's feelings. They have a reason to look for others who affirm them and make them even feel superior.

STEER STRAIGHT WHEREVER POSSIBLE

A manipulator's actions typically vary according to the situation they're in. For instance, a manipulator may speak rudely to one person, and act respectfully towards another the next moment. When you see these extremes frequently in a person, it would be advisable to stay away from them. And you have to communicate with this guy. That will prevent you from becoming a deceptive victim.

One way to identify a manipulator is to see how a person is behaving in different circumstances and before different people.

Although we all have a sense of this sort of social distinction, some psychological manipulators seem to dwell in extremes habitually, being highly polite to one person, and gross to another - or helpless at one moment, and fiercely violent at another. If you frequently experience this form of behavior from an adult, keep a healthy distance away, and avoid interacting with the person unless you have to. As described earlier, there are nuanced and deep-seated causes for persistent psychological abuse. Saving them is not your job.

There are some circumstances in which you can't fully leave a relationship-usually when that person is a parent or an extended family member. You probably cannot go cold turkey unless the individual causes serious harm or psychological damage. Next, you need to accept this person completely for who they are and change your relationship standards accordingly. If they were someone you needed validation from before, then you would have to quit looking for their validation. Recognize that their advice is not something you need in your life. When they keep offering it, you can thank them for it, and then politely dump it. When setting these limits, be as discreet as you can, and do not tell the other person you are setting them apart. Creating this shift at your end will take some time, and when you get upset with the other person in the process, you will have to deal with their reaction on top of that.

Knowing this will drain your energy a little bit, set limits around the time you spend with that person. If you've been hanging out every Saturday with your manipulating mother-in-law, cut it down to once a month and plan something for that day so that there is a definite end time for your hangout.

CALL THEM OUT ON THEIR ACTIONS

Manipulators are always difficult to deal with, but the worst arediscreet manipulators. They will stay cool as a cucumber when confronted, and yet rigid and unbending. You may start to get frustrated when you start seeing their faulty reasoning. When you keep fighting with them, you'll find it hard not to raise your voice a bit. You will start looking like the irrational one, and they will try to take back control in remaining calm, based on their "maturity."

Defending yourself is tempting and trying to get the other person to see what is going on. But a true manipulator will not change their tune, and the more you give in to that urge to protect yourself, the more they will twist your words more. It will not be long before you get stuck in this twisted web of myths and false expectations. If you are in a situation with a true manipulator, the two goals for any conflict that is taking place should be to resolve and leave, whether that means leaving the current conversation or exiting the relationship. Avoid threats, accusations, losing patience, accusing the other person of coercion, or become excessively emotional. Stick to honest, factual, and respectful declarations when you speak.

Some things require a high degree of intelligence, flexibility, or self-discipline when dealing with a manipulative person. You might not have the self-control to react without losing your temper and making things worse. If that's the case, accept this about yourself and take extra steps to avoid a tense confrontation (invite a mediator into the conversation, for example, or send an email instead of meeting in person, so you have time to think through what you say).

For me, it can cause a bit of tension to deal with someone who loses their temper. I needed to have a friend with me to feel secure in circumstances where there were a lot of blow-up risks. However, much as I wished I could handle the conflict myself, I realized that I wasn't quite in a position to do so. I would have felt a lot of needless discomforts if I had failed to acknowledge this about myself because of my decision to act better than I was. Wouldn't you be better at handling the problem than you are? Others will be attacking the vulnerable points and trying to make it seem like the problem will be easier for you to deal with than it is. Do not equate your reaction to someone else's reaction in one case.

IGNORE WHAT THEY DO AND SAY

It is intended to ignore the dishonest men. These people flip flop over things, they're slippery when you try to keep them accountable, they promise support that never comes, they're always making you feel guiltyeverything you don't want in person. The greatest mistake you can make when dealing with a dishonest person is trying to correct him or her. You sink deeper into their pit, by correcting them. Humans will use anger and misunderstanding to lure you into a confrontation. We want to make you feel nervous so that they can see how you tick. When they learn the triggering factors, you will use them to affect your actions. A smarter approach is to ignore them entirely. Only erase them from your life if you can't delete them instantly-even if they're a supervisor, coworker, or member of the family and then carry on doing your own thing anyway.

TOUCH THEIR CENTRE OF GRAVITY

Manipulative people actively take advantage of their tactics against you. Through your enemies, they will become enemies, and turn them against you. They will dangle some small reward in front of you and make you chase it relentlessly-they're going to take it away any time you get close to it. You will forever keep past acts up against you and on and on. Avoid letting those who exploit you, by using their tactics against you. Switch the tables instead. Build your plan and hit them where it hurts. When you are forced to deal with a dishonest person who, no matter how hard you try to avoid them, tries to make your life miserable, your only choice is to find their center of gravity and destroy it. This center may be associates, followers, or subordinates to the deceptive individual. It may be a high-level talent or advanced knowledge of a particular area. They can manage it as a particular resource.

Figure out what their center of gravity is and make it yours anyway. Creating alliances with those close to them, hiring people to replace them with their skill sets and knowledge base, or siphoning away their precious assets. This will throw them off balance and push them to concentrate on managing their life, not yours.

BELIEVE IN YOUR DECISION

You know better than anyone else what is best for your future. Many people are going around asking for the views of other people on anything. "What do I want to do with my life?""What am I fantastic at?""Where am I, then?", avoid searching for other people's validationand describe it yourself. Define yourself. Believe in yourself. What distinguishes winners from losers is not the ability to listen to other people's opinions; it's the ability to listen to one's own opinions. You prevent dishonest people from influencing your life by setting up your values and keeping them tightly onto them. This will serve as a firewall to your convictions, keeping manipulators ostracized and out of your way.

TRY NOT TO FIT RIGHT IN

Keep reinventing yourself. One myth is the belief that continuity is somehow admirable or related to achievement. Manipulative people want you to be consistent so that they can count on you to advance their agendas. They want you to show up at 9 am every day and work at minimum wage for them. We want you to come home on time and make them feel good about themselves and clean the house.

Consistent assembly lines. The prison is uniform. Consistency is how they trap you in a shell. It's their way of manipulating you. The only way to stop being exploited is by consciously going against all the barriers other people seek to create for you. Let go of trying to blend in. Instead, lookto stand out. Act different in some way, and never remain the same for too long. By design, personal growth needs a lack of consistency. Constant change is expected to achieve constant reinvention.

AVOID CONCESSION

Guilt is an emotion of no use, but this is a powerful tool. Guilt is one of those weapons that would be used against you by dishonest men. They will make you feel bad for past defeats and small mistakes, or they will make you feel guilty for being overconfident and prideful. They'll use it against you if you spend time feeling happy or sure of yourself. One will never feel too good about themselves; they would claim. Another tool that is being used against you by manipulators is doubt. They will work to instill within you a sense of self-doubt-doubts about your ability and your worth. Their ultimate goal is to take you off balance and make you second guess yourself. Within this state of confusion, manipulators gain control. Their power is getting greater and they are twice as likely to convince you to compromise on your principles, ambitions, and yourself.

Simple solution-avoid feeling guilty. When it comes to your own life, you owe nothing to anyone. You deserve to feel good about yourself and to be stunned by your achievements. You deserve to have a good sense of confidence and self-belief in what you do. It is neither moral nor enlightened to compromise on either of these issues. This is then the path to self-destruction.

NEVER ASK FOR PERMISSION

Asking for forgiveness is better than asking for permission. The problem is that we have been conditioned to ask for permission constantly. As a boy, we had to ask for everything we wanted — to be fed, changed, and burped. We had to ask permission to go to the bathroom, and we had to wait to eat lunch at a designated time and wait for our turn to play with toys. As a result, most people expect to seek permission.

Employees around the world are waiting for a promotion and waiting for their turn to talk. Most are so used to being chosen that they sit in meetings in silence, afraid to talk out of turn or even lift their hands. It's a different way of living.

What if you did it what you wanted to, whenever you want? And what if you quit being too worried about politeness and feel relaxed with others? What if, instead, you live your life exactly the way you want to live it? These are all things you can do whenever you want.

Manipulative people want you to feel constrained by some abstract law or principle that says you can't behave freely without consulting an authority figure or a party. The reality is that at any given moment, you can miss this feeling of confinement. You will continue living a completely different life today than you lived yesterday. Your decision is yours.

BUILD A GREATER SENSE OF MISSION

Destiny driven people aren't easily fooled. The reason manipulators in this world tend to prosper is that so many people lead a purposeless life. If there is no reason in your life, you cannot believe anything. They will do anything. Because, somehow, nothing matters. People who lack intent waste time. There is no rhyme or explanation behind how they live their lives. We don't know where to go, or why they are here. They remain busy to avoid the desperate feeling of emptiness growing inside them. This profession and loneliness empower deceptive individuals.

Every minute, a sucker is born. When you are constantly distracted, consuming pointless stuff, trying to stay busy-you are the sucker. By peddling meaningless knowledge and events, manipulators manipulate purposeless people. The only way to escape this, is by cultivating a sense of destiny. Destiny is doing away with distraction. The manipulators can't hurt you because you think for yourself. They cannot confuse you or lead you astray.

TAKE NEW OPPORTUNITIES

The universe wants to put your eggs in one bowl. People all around you ask you to lock yourself in on decisions such as a mortgage, a car payment, a secure relationship, a single position at the office. They want you staked down to a single choice for the rest of your life. Nowadays, it is also looked down upon for being optimistic. Staying hungry is also seen as a sign of weakness. Why can't you just be happy with what you have? Why should you be so greedy? If you show a desire for more, this is what dishonest people would ask you. They will call you vain, greedy, prideful. They'll make you feel cold and uncomfortable like you're heartless and inhumane. The reality is that they want to keep you in your place. They want you to stay at the same job and spend the rest of your life living in the same place. They want you and the structures they control to remain dependent upon them.

The only way to stay autonomous is to look for new possibilities and build new ones actively. Continue applying for new jobs, continue to start at new companies, developing new partnerships, and seeking new experiences.

AVOID BEING AN INFANT

When you get fooled by someone, shame on them. When you're fooled by someone ten times, you're an idiot. Avoid letting manipulators walk all over you. Nobody feels sorry for you, and you're always being humiliated. Have enough self-consciousness and reverence for yourself to say no to dishonest men.

You cannot just walk around life, blaming the troubles on others. You cannot simply walk away from the people trying to control you, either. Yes, some people are negative and manipulative. And yes, these people will try to use you. Yet, that doesn't mean that you have a free pass to make mistakes. Without your permission, no-one can control you. You are to blame for your achievements and defeats. If others outstrip you, it's your fault, not theirs, so be smart. Learn from your wrongs. You don't want to fall victim to the same slippery person again and again. Slice them free. Remove them from your life. Commit to connecting yourself with like-minded people who will not be exploiting you.

BETTING ON YOURSELF

Take a gamble on the one thing in life that you can control yourself. Too many people restrict themselves to considering only external factors when making difficult decisions. They consider the financial consequences of a situation and its relationships. Yet they fail to acknowledge the impact on their satisfaction and sense of self-worth their choice would have. As a result, when they should be taking chances on themselves, they take chances on other people. Then, they wonder why they are unhappy.

If you just take chances on strangers and things, you put yourself at the mercy of those people and things. It makes you weak and ready to be exploited. You should take chances on yourself instead. In any tough situation you find yourself facing, don't ask questions like, "Who's the right one to side with?" or"What choice would be more likely to succeed?" rather, say,"What am I most likely to do?" so go out and do that. For example, if you face an opportunity to start your own company or keep working at the same dead-end job, don't keep the job just because the pay is stable. Don't just leave because the relationships are slightly unpleasant. You are betting on external factors when you do so, which is a mistake. Betting on yourself is a safer plan.

167

You would never regret making a bet on yourself. You will, of course, have to take full responsibility for any mistakes that you make. Sure, you need to stick to a higher standard. Yet you, too, must be solely responsible for your victories. You will continue to rise and achieve greater and higher rates of success.

STOP GETTING EMOTIONALLY ATTACHED TO THEM

All you do with a manipulator is fake. Every fight you have been through is your fault. Manipulation will wreak havoc on your feelings. You go from crying to being furious in a short period of time, then to feeling guilty and indignant. Then you feelsorry you did not stick up for yourself. You are ashamed to let them do that to you again, and your emotions are more stable once you've left a manipulator.

Life is a journey into an adventure. On the way, many people come to give us company at various times, for a certain amount of time and leave after they play their part in our lives. There is no problem with the people coming and going, but the difficulties occur when you are emotionally attached to the people and feel powerless, tense, and worried when the relationship ends, especially with an emotional manipulator. Therefore, if you want to stay healthy and make progress in life, you need to resolve the emotional connection as soon as possible. There is no doubt that some individuals will become the driving force for you to move towards the path you have chosen but when being separated from them, you should be careful not to get distracted. You need to make judicious use of the relationships. Be attached to individuals with a detached approach and take care of them to create a confident atmosphere. However, when you push them out of your life for being a manipulator withanother relationship waiting for you, do not be dependent on that person for your growth by stopping your life. You need to re-focus on your journey, leavingbehind memories.

Handling emotional connection measures the degree of sophistication of one's journey down the desired direction, and its gravity. Treat yourself to the moments you share with friends. Learn from them, love them, and look after them, but don't make them your walking sticks. Much of the time, people are usually afraid to lose anyone because of their incapacity to go on in life alone. So, if you dare walk alone on the chosen path, you no longer have to be dependent on emotional connections.

INSPIRING THEM

Using all the experience you've acquired to become your best self, help others to become their best. If you are having trouble improving their behavior, work with a counselor. It can be very difficult to change their behavior, and you may not be able to do it on your own. A psychologist or therapist may help him recognize habits that need to be altered and discuss the feelings that are behind him. These will also help him develop new, healthy behaviors.

TELL THEM "YOU'RE OK."

This begins with you not responding to their techniques anymore. If you don't want to something, you say "no," or you speak your mind even though they don't like it. Work on feeling okay with how negatively they may react. When they're not yours, don't pick them up.

You can only keep your act under control. That's crucial because you won't be able to alter a manipulator's behavior, however, you can avoid being their victim. That happens when you start saying, "no." The first step in breaking the cycle is to recognize that they manipulate us because we allow it and do not refuse to be manipulated. Manipulators are good at what they do, so watch out for their reaction. You would probably say or do things that tug at the heartstrings. Stand firm in saying "no," realizing we are taking the first step to free ourselves from their power.

LET GO OF NASTY RELATIONSHIPS

Toxic partnerships can be hard to let go of. Many people find themselves caught in a cycle of returning to relationships that are not good for them. This just creates a cycle of hurt and grief. Toxic relationships can be let go of. Psychologists have worked with people who have had this issue to be able to write a whole handbook about it. The very first step to getting out of a toxic relationship is admitting to yourself that the relationship isn't perfect. You can try and note down explanations of the sign indicating a toxic relationship. It's called 'cognitive dissonance' if you notice that uncomfortable feeling in the back of your mind, and it's your brain trying to protect you from what you know is true. Take note of the things that make you feel this way in a relationship. The first step is to recognize that your relationship is toxic. You have to be conscious of all the things that affect you before you can truly be free.

Relationships are a side lane. Two people are involved in the relationship, meaning that two people are involved in all the disagreements, arguments, and behavior. You cannot fully take the blame yourself. If you blame yourself for all of the relationship problems, you'll find yourself going back to trying to fix them. Recognize that both parties are sometimes at fault for a dysfunctional relationship. Recognize your responsibilities, but your responsibilities alone. Within a toxic relationship, you don't need to be concernedwith anyone else's issues. There's no need to hoist it on yourself because you aren't to blame.

Some of the best things you can do while trying to let go of a controlling partner is to cut off communication. Keeping in touch would just make letting go harder. This involves seeking outtoxic people that are no longer in your life by scrolling through their social media or questioning how they are doing through mutual friends. You should still follow your intuition when it comes to cutting people out of your life, according to Sarah Newman, M.A. Although it may sound drastic, Newman advises loosening the bonds when it comes to a toxic relationship. You need to be in a position to move on, where you can feel optimistic about the lack of touch, rather than pain.

Mariana Bockarova, Ph.D., says that closure is one of the best things to move on from a manipulative and broken relationship. Bockarova understands that closure will help people reconstruct their whole lives safely and positively. Thus, one way to help you let go of a toxic relationship is to find closure. Healing comes from inside for many people by considering all the ways the relationship went wrong in the first place. Writing one more letter or making the other party recognize the toxicity will provide closure for some. Whatever it is, the closure might help you move on.

The most important thing in quitting and letting go of an abusive relationship is having someone there to catch you if you fall. It can be unsettling to let go, especially if it is a long-term one. Keep in contact with friends and relatives who will support you through the more stressful moments. This will also help to keep you accountable when it comes to not reaching out those you've cut off. Aid networks are essential in allowing dysfunctional partnerships to go away. Don't fear reaching out to people who love you the most.

DEVELOP A STRONG MINDSET

Although one toxic person may use coercion and lies, another may have recourse to intimidation and incivility. If you're not careful, it can take a serious toll on your life because of people like this. Nevertheless, mentally healthy people deal skillfully with manipulative people. They refuse to give away their strength, and no matter who surrounds them, they continue to be their best self.

Putting a label on emotions reduces their intensity. So, whether you feel sad, nervous, frustrated, or afraid, confess it — at least to yourself. Pay attention also to how those emotions can affect your choices. You can be less likely to take chances when you are feeling nervous. You may get more impulsive when you're excited. Increasing the understanding of the feelings will reduce the risk that you will make emotionally driven, unreasonable decisions.

Listing your emotions is just part of the fight — you need skills to control your emotions as well. Think of your current abilities to cope. Should you eat something when you're nervous? Should you drink to keep yourself calm? When you're mad, will you show it to your friends? If you're anxious, will you stay at home? These conventional strategies can make you feel better right now, but they will make you feel worse in the long run. Search for long-term coping strategies that are perfect for you. Keep in mind that what works for one person doesn't always work for another, and you need to figure out what's best for you to manage your emotions. Experimenting with various coping mechanisms to figure out what works for you, deep breathing, exercising, meditating, reading, painting, and spending time in nature are only a few techniques that could help.

The way you think has an impact on how you feel and how you behave. You are deprived of intellectual energy by saying things like, "I can't take this," or "I'm such an idiot." Pay attention to what you think. You'll probably note recurring trends and themes. Maybe you're telling yourself things you feel uncomfortable about doing. Or maybe you're telling yourself you're not in control of your life.

Respond with something more constructive to the unproductive and unreasonable feelings. Instead of saying, "I'm going to screw this up," think, "This is my chance to shine, and I'm going to do my best." Changing the interactions you're having with yourself can be the most instrumental thing you can do to improve your existence. Changing your attitude is the only way to teach your brain to think differently. Do tough things — and keep doing them even though you don't think you should. You will be demonstrating to yourself that you are stronger than you think. Set up healthy daily habits too. Practice appreciation, exercise, get plenty of sleep and follow a balanced diet for the brain and body to be at its best. Seek out individuals who inspire you to be your best and create an atmosphere that helps you develop a balanced lifestyle.

Many positive habits won't work if you practice them alongside your bad habits. It is like eating donuts on a treadmill while you're running. Pay attention to your bad habits (we all have them) that rob you of the mental strength. Whether you feel bad for yourself or envy the success of other people, it takes only one or two to keep you stuck in life. Once you realize your bad habits, spend your energy replacing them with healthier alternatives. You will then be able to step out of the hamster wheel and actively work towards your goals.

Just as it takes time and practice to become physically strong, it takes dedication to build mental strength. The key to feeling your best and reaching your most significant potential is to build mental muscle.

GIVE YOURSELF CONSTRUCTIVE SELF-APPRAISAL ALL DAY LONG

An emotional manipulator will tarnish your mood, so make sure you restore yourself during the day with uplifting self-talks. Each of us has a set of messages that keep playing in our minds over and over. Our responses to life and its circumstances are represented by this internal dialog or personal commentary. One way to recognize, encourage, and maintain optimism, hope, and happiness is to fill our minds with optimistic self-talking consciously. Far too often, because of our manipulative partner, the self-talk pattern that we have formed is negative. We recall the derogatory things our friends, parents, siblings, or teachers told us as children. We remember other children's adverse reactions, which undermined the way we felt about ourselves. Such messages have been playing in our minds over the years, strengthening our feelings of rage, fear, guilt, and hopelessness.

Some of the most important approaches used in dealing with those suffering from depression are to determine the root of these messages and to work with the individual to "overwrite" them deliberately. If a person learned he was worthless as a child, we'd show him how special he is. If a person has learned to expect disasters and catastrophic events while growing up, we will teach her a better way to predict the future.

Check the exercise below. Within your head, write down some of the negative thoughts that hinder your desire to resolve your circumstance. Whenever possible, be precise, and include everyone you know who contributed to it. Now, take a moment to consciously combat the negative messages in your life with constructive truths. Don't give up when you're not quick to find them, because thereare always truths for every negative message which will help override them. So keep looking until you find them.

You can get a negative message replaying in your mind if you make a mistake. You might have been told as a child, "You're never going to amount to anything," or "You can't do anything right." When you make a mistake, and you will because we all do - you can choose to overwrite that message with a positive one, such as "I choose to accept and grow from my mistake" or "As I learn from my mistakes, I become a better person." Good self-conversation isn't self-deception. It's not looking at circumstances through rose tinted glasses, instead, it is about acknowledging the truth in situations and within you. One of the fundamental truths is that you will be making mistakes. It is unfair to expect perfection in yourself or someone else. It's also unrealistic to expect no difficulties in life, whether by your actions or by pure circumstances.

When adverse events or mistakes occur, positive self-talk is aimed at bringing the positive out of the negative to help you do better, go further, or simply move forward. The practice of constructive self-talk is also the mechanism that helps you to discover in any given situation the hidden happiness, hope, and joy.

STAY OBSERVANT

If you know that you are a target, you must be observant at all times. In other words, we all need to stay observant. Everybody is a prime target of manipulation. People will come to you to take advantage of your situation. Staying observant means that you can look at people and read their intentions. As we have observed, NLP professionals will use their extraction techniques to try and gauge our thoughts and beliefs. If you wish to stop those individuals from controlling your life and thinking process, you must stay aware. Always try to remember that there is someone out there who may be looking to take control of your thoughts.

BE SECRETIVE

Do not be a person who gives out your information to everyone. A manipulative person can only control you if they know something about you. If the manipulator does not have any information about you, they may not have any valid reasons to control your life. If you want to stay on your feet and stop all the people who come to your life to control you, you must learn to stop them by blocking their quest to gain knowledge about your life.

LEARN TO CONTROL YOUR EMOTIONS

NLP experts do not need you to speak for them to gather information. NLP experts rely more on the emotional clues that you send out during conversations. You must learn how to control your expressive and physiological aspects of emotions. The physiological aspects of emotion include the bodily changes that take place when you are emotional. For instance, the sweating of hands when you are anxious or afraid. Such physiological changes may sell you out to the person who wants to get more information to manipulate you. The expressive aspect of emotions includes bodily actions that you display when you are emotional. A good example would be running away when you are afraid. Although you may choose to stay, the actions of running away or choosing to fight are an expressive part of your emotions that NLP experts may use to gather more information about your past.

AVOID ISOLATION

Try as much as possible to ensure that you do not allow a manipulative person to isolate you. When you are isolated, you are weak and vulnerable. Most manipulative people gain control during moments of weakness, such as isolation.

Conclusion

There has been lots of discussion about dark psychology, how and in which situations it is practiced most commonly and what the factors hidden behind it are. This is also considered to be a dark side of human nature, which is seldom exposed. Every human being, no matter how nice and positive they are, are always going to be evil in someone else's eyes. For the person whom you made suffer, you are evil, even if you deny it. Every person must evaluate him or herself and see if any of the hazardous or negative elements are found in them. You have to keep fighting your dark side so that it does not take control over you completely. Once you know to keep off that side, you will be able to identify it in others as well and can prevent yourself from falling prey to it. One must be aware of its indications and related signs so that people who have the qualities of dark psychology can be avoided. If you have fallen prey to dark psychology, then there is a chance for you to regain normality by assessing and evaluating yourself or by seeking medical advice.

Remember that deception is not always practiced on other people. We can often self-deceive to preserve our self-esteem. Telling ourselves that we can achieve certain goals when all the evidence points to the fact that we can't, is a healthy form of deception, but self-deception can lead to serious delusions.

Whatever happens in the novice stages of your path to becoming a master of manipulation and persuasion, you must remember your end goal. Ask yourself in the beginning why you want to do this and keep coming back to that when it gets hard. Never give up; you are to master these skills.

I hope that through this book, you have realized that brainwashing, manipulation, and persuasion depends greatly on an authoritative command of words. You might be able to list twenty manipulation techniques from memory; you may be able to get someone with little psychic resistance to go with your ideas.

You may have gotten to the end of the book — and you may have all the knowledge necessary to manipulate people — but you are just beginning when it comes to putting this all into practice.

Also, remember manipulation is classified into positive and negative (Egocentric and Malicious). The study shows how toavoid negative manipulators and try as hard as possible to stay in your lane. Work on the positive aspect of manipulation to help yourself and help others — best of luck!